Abnormal

How to Train Yourself to Think Differently and Permanently Overcome Evil Thoughts

Dan Desmarques

22 Lions

Abnormal: How to Train Yourself to Think Differently and Permanently Overcome Evil Thoughts

Written by Dan Desmarques

Copyright © 2024 (Second Edition), by Dan Desmarques. All rights reserved.

Copyright © 2022 (First Edition), by Dan Desmarques. All rights reserved.

No part of this publication may be reproduced or transmitted in any form or by any means, electronic or mechanical, including photocopy, recording, or any information storage and retrieval system now known or to be invented, without permission in writing from the publisher, except by a reviewer who wishes to quote brief passages in connection with a review written for inclusion in a magazine, newspaper, or broadcast.

Contents

	Introduction	IX
1.	Chapter 1 - The Evolution of Covert Antisocial Behavior	1
2.	Chapter 2 - Exposing the Lies That Divide Society	5
3.	Chapter 3 - Projection and Perception in a Psychopathic World	9
4.	Chapter 4 - How Narcissists Target the Exceptional	13
5.	Chapter 5 - The Roots of Racism and Xenophobia	17
6.	Chapter 6 - How Fear and Conformity Enslave Us	21
7.	Chapter 7 - The Evolution of Perception	25
8.	Chapter 8 - How Collective Ignorance Shapes Our World	29
9.	Chapter 9 - The Spiral of Avoidance	33
10.	Chapter 10 - Mental Enslavement in a Controlled System	37
11.	Chapter 11 - The Unimportance of What People Say	41
12.	Chapter 12 - How Perception Shapes Our Lives	45

13.	Chapter 13 - Decision Making and the Illusion of Logic	49
14.	Chapter 14 - Working for a Better World	53
15.	Chapter 15 - The Resistance to Change and Evolution	57
16.	Chapter 16 - The Misalignment of Expectations	61
17.	Chapter 17 - The Isolation of the Developed	65
18.	Chapter 18 - The Silent Driver of Wars and Prejudice	69
19.	Chapter 19 - The Irrational Forces That Shape Our World	73
20.	Chapter 20 - The Psychopathic Roots of War and Conflict	77
21.	Chapter 21 - Personal Interests and the Future of the Planet	81
22.	Chapter 22 - Breaking Free from Cultural Norms and Evolving Consciousness	85
23.	Chapter 23 - Cultural Toxicity and the Corruption of the Self	89
24.	Chapter 24 - Debunking False Paradigms and Embracing Opportunity	93
25.	Chapter 25 - The Decline of Social Values and the Rise of Complacency	97
26.	Chapter 26 - Transcending Dualities and the Stagnation of Religion	101

27.	Chapter 27 - The Perverse Cycle of Modern Slavery and the Way Out	107
28.	Chapter 28 - The Reality of Poor Nations and Miserable Cultures	113
29.	Chapter 29 - The Hard Truth About Parental Responsibility and Success	119
30.	Chapter 30 - Making Informed Decisions in a World of Psychopaths	123
31.	Chapter 31 - The Value of Discretion and Strategic Investment	129
32.	Chapter 32 - Focus on Quality and the People Who Appreciate It	133
33.	Chapter 33 - Finding True Faith Beyond Organized Belief	137
34.	Chapter 34 - Understanding the Levels of Social Integration	141
35.	Chapter 35 - Healing Through Connection and Externalization	145
36.	Glossary of Terms	149
37.	Book Review Request	153
38.	About the Author	155
39.	Also Written by the Author	157
40.	About the Publisher	167

Introduction

In a world where aggression and power often overshadow love and compassion, "Abnormal: How to Train Yourself to Think Differently and Permanently Overcome Evil Thoughts" offers a transformative journey into understanding the complexities of human behavior and societal dynamics. This book explores the roots of psychopathy, societal pressures, and the dualities that shape our perceptions and interactions. It challenges readers to break free from conventional thinking and encourages a path of self-discovery and evolution.

Through a comprehensive exploration of individual neurology and societal influences, the book reveals how fear, shame, and societal expectations can lead to covert antisocial behavior and a predatory mindset. It emphasizes the importance of education, self-awareness, and the courage to think differently as keys to overcoming these destructive patterns. Readers will gain insight into the evolutionary development of the human mind, the influence of cultural and personal experiences, and the power of introspection. By understanding the underlying motives and fears that drive human actions, this book empowers individuals to transcend societal norms and embrace a more evolved way of thinking.

More than a guide to personal growth, "Abnormal" is a call to action for societal change, urging readers to contribute to a world where cooperation and empathy prevail over division and competition. Whether you're looking to understand the intricacies of human psychology or transform your own life, this book provides the tools and perspectives needed to navigate and thrive in a complex world.

Chapter 1 - The Evolution of Covert Antisocial Behavior

You have probably spent most of your life wondering why so many people are evil and even jealous of others, and why this happens to those who have done nothing wrong and spend most of their time focused on their own existence and the survival of their family. Much of the evil in the world is attributed to mysterious causes, often isolated in the realm of religion, and psychopathy does not get the attention it deserves when we analyze it from a broader perspective or when we see its many implications in our daily lives. But everything can be simplified within a certain evolutionary path that reveals our hidden motives, ambitions, fears, and reasons. To do this, we need a better understanding of individual neurology and how it applies to the many facets of evil in the world today.

In a world of self-destructive tendencies and abnormal views of reality, where aggression and power are often more valued and revered than love and compassion, the only way out is to use a social mask. People then have to pretend to be someone they're not in order to be respected and fit into society. This state of mind will obviously lead to social anxiety, so when people are depressed they will make more effort to hide it, even smiling more than normal and at unusual things. This is because they are afraid of being discriminated against. However, because people want to be part of a society that makes them anxious, many then develop what is called covert antisocial behavior, which means they will lie more, cheat on others, and generally do whatever they can to survive and win in what they perceive as a wild competition to get more.

This predatory mindset comes from the very state of being a victim, which means it is a compensation for the fear of being prey in what they see as a dual world - a two-dimensional reality. In essence, depression and anger put people in a situation where their perception of life is reduced to a very low level, which then affects how they see themselves and others, but most importantly, how they behave.

Of course, when such psychotic individuals act this way towards other people, it doesn't take long for them to suffer the consequences of their betrayals and lies, which as a result, and because they cannot reflect on their own behavior, will lead them even deeper into this reptilian mindset of seeking power over other people in order to oppress them and survive. Survival is perceived by this person as a mechanism by which he diminishes the potential of others in order to make himself more able to prey upon and lie to them. Those he preys upon may then begin to perceive reality in the same dual way, which is why there are so many people who hold society down and do not allow it to evolve.

If a person remains in a fearful state of mind long enough, anger and more depression will follow, eventually leading the individual to suicidal thoughts. Everything the individual perceives outside of himself ends up being a reflection of his inner world, even though there is no correlation between what is happening and what he perceives might be happening. The psychotic state correlates with a lack of discrimination and self-control over one's thoughts, which means that the person is more disturbed by simple and ordinary problems, but also more likely to rationalize what is happening as a negative attack on his existence.

This description is a summary of what is happening all over the planet, and for many it is so common that it can even be considered normal. Some have labeled these traits as part of a certain reptilian brain as opposed to a mammalian brain, and while this type of comparison may facilitate our understanding, it is misleading. The human mind must be understood within an evolutionary trajectory that manifests not according to what we see now, but according to the full potential of an individual. This means that many people still live with the thought patterns of a caveman or someone from centuries past. There are many reasons for this: it may be related to past lives, lack of education, cultural aspects, childhood trauma, or a combination of these elements.

Although some experiences affect us more than others, how they affect us also depends on how we respond, and our responses are correlated with everything else we have experienced before. But with education and training, a person can become better, recover from their previous mental state, and evolve to a higher way of thinking. This requires a certain amount of cooperation on the part of the individual, and therein lies the problem, for someone who sees the world as a threat is unlikely to accept help or see help as a beneficial thing.

Chapter 2 - Exposing the Lies That Divide Society

The healthier a person is, the more willing they are to be helped, but also the less likely they are to need outside intervention because they are already helping themselves and doing so safely. In this process you will see that people tend to align themselves with a certain path: At the bottom you will see a person who is obsessed with their survival as a body. This means looking at the world in two dimensions, only two options, two divisions: me and them, hunter or hunted, attacker or defender, aggressor or victim. But what is very interesting to observe is that the people who propose an analysis of the world based on dualities - while presenting themselves as helpful to others - are actually doing the opposite, leading society deeper into this false dogma of "me versus them".

If we want to understand the truth, we must look for those who propose models that integrate society in a constant planetary evolution. Among these theories we will find the following: The people at the top of our evolution are not obsessed with getting, but rather interested in giving. They are the ones who understand that the world can only progress through cooperation and a synergistic combination of efforts, just as we can observe in nature. In fact, you can look at nature from a binary point of view, predator and prey, or you can look at it from a broader perspective and realize that the whole system works to sustain itself.

Of course, animals don't know what they're doing, just as many people don't know why they do things the way they do, but there is a balance that keeps nature as it is, and that balance is disrupted when one element is removed. It is the same with human society. If it does not cooperate, wars follow, greed and destruction follow, and the result of all this is death and the impossibility of progress. In fact, the stupidest people on this planet are those who say that money is not important and that all people are good if they are treated with respect. They obviously don't know what planet they live on or how life works. We need both wealth and realism to rationalize the possibility of a future instead of excuses for a self-destructive present.

If we can understand why society as a whole is not organized for evolution, but rather according to the perverse mindset of those who view it from the bottom of our evolutionary scale - thinking that evolution is a matter of luck, an accident that blows in the wind and happens to be caught by some - then we can look at our own existence very differently, because we will realize that most of what we are told is a lie, an illusion designed to keep us in line with the common psychotic mindset of the many.

Imagine that you live in a very primitive era, and everyone tells you that you must learn to throw spears to keep enemy tribes from invading your land, and that the only way you will ever survive is to hunt wild animals. You will spend your whole life thinking that this is your reality. You will never try anything else. Then when you see someone living differently, like a former tribal member who decided to break away from this insanity and built a boat and lives by fishing and farming, you will say that he is crazy. Until you realize that you are undeveloped, you will not see that this other person is more developed than you are. To see such a madman as evolved, you have to realize that you are not evolved.

This is what happens in society today. People think that those who are more evolved are crazy. They are called greedy, cynical, lost, or just plain arrogant. If you look at the words that are chosen to describe the people who are rejected for being too evolved, you will see that these words all have to do with things that people can't do: They are practical, creative, adventurous risk-takers who seek out new possibilities and are not afraid to think differently.

The differences between people are easy to see in the way they structure their perceptions. For example, if you read a lot and join a group of people who don't, they may think you read too much or that your conversations are boring. But if you don't read at all and join a club of readers, they'll think you're too stupid to talk to. And what if you read more than the person in front of you, but he thinks you are stupid? Of course he will discredit you, judge you negatively, invalidate you, and devalue everything you say, looking for reasons to rationalize his thoughts and keep his identity and self-image intact, preferably of superiority over you. He will say that you are lying and that you are crazy. This is the state of mind of many people in this world.

Chapter 3 - Projection and Perception in a Psychopathic World

There is nothing wrong with seeing things as they are, but instead perceiving them as what we think they are, because this is forcing our perceptions of reality onto the real world, rather than analyzing the world as it is. This inability to see reality for what it is is very evident in the way people insult each other because the vast majority of the population projects their own problems, insecurities, and limitations onto others while failing to see that the things they observe are a reflection of themselves and not reality itself.

For example, a man in his late 40s who still lives with his mother and can't get a job called me childish and said I didn't have a mature way of looking at reality; a fat man who can barely move said I couldn't punch a paper bag; a man who tries to evade taxes by lying about the sources of his income called me a criminal; A man without a college degree said I didn't know how to do research; a man with a very ugly girlfriend said I was probably a virgin because I was single; an author who spent his whole life writing books that didn't sell said I wasn't a real author like him because he published with the most prestigious French publisher; A very ignorant man who keeps failing with his business ideas said it was impossible to make money online and that I was lying about my job; a very fat woman made fun of my skin color and said I didn't look like a European; a Spanish man who looks like an Arab himself said I looked like an Arab in a demeaning tone of voice; A psychopathic woman who struggles with mental illness said I sounded crazy; a woman who failed to publish her first novel and gave up on her dreams said I didn't look like a real writer; a narcissist who was once diagnosed with mental illness called me crazy for asking him to apologize for his past behavior.

These are all real examples of the many people I have met who have insulted me and the kinds of things they say. You only have to look at them with the same words they use to understand that they are talking about themselves. Moreover, the insults are so at odds with my own reality that I would have to question my sanity to believe them. This is also why it is hard to get angry at these people when what they are saying has more to do with themselves than the person in front of them. It is as if they are mirroring their own problems as loudly as they can into a need for salvation. They insult with phrases that describe them much more than anyone else, and in many cases have no correlation to the person they are trying to insult.

These are also examples of extreme levels of psychopathy, although they are very common in our society. These people can only pretend to be normal in a world that knows little about mental illness. In fact, they are more likely to insult sane people because they can see clearly behind their mask. The most insane people in the world will always target the most sane people for fear of exposure and shame. Fear and shame are the emotions that most dominate and terrorize the psychopathic mind, and you can easily make them feel weak by exposing these two traits in them. You do this by looking at their weaknesses and mentioning them repeatedly, because their accusations are just smoke to distract you from the real problem - themselves.

Another word for this tactic is gaslighting, precisely because it is designed to make you doubt your own sanity by reversing the roles. They want you to think you are them so they can be you. It sounds crazy because it is, and very crazy people think this way, and they are the majority. But the other reason mentally ill people switch roles in an interaction, interestingly enough, is because they can't empathize with the other person. They will switch roles in a conversation and blame you for things they do because they can't understand your point of view, and the reason they can't has to do with their own fear and shame. They are stuck in their own mental patterns and obsessed with survival.

Fear and shame make people introverted, focused on their own need to survive at all costs, regardless of the needs of others. But this is not the same as saying someone is shy. An introvert in this case is a person who has internalized his own view of the world and can't change it when interacting with reality. Therefore, this person becomes a narcissist, not because he thinks he is better than others, but because he knows he is worse than everyone else. This narcissism is the mask created to distract, humiliate, and belittle others. And they do these things because they can't see themselves behind the mask, and they can't tolerate anyone else seeing them for who they are.

Chapter 4 - How Narcissists Target the Exceptional

It is just as easy to compliment a person as it is to insult them, because both qualities are often visible. The things people most want to hide are their weaknesses, while the things they most expose and talk about are their best qualities. But insecurities cause people to belittle others as a self-defense mechanism. It is as if they would sacrifice another's well-being to protect their own, just as a very greedy and selfish person would do, which is why the same traits are often present in the same people. The greedy, the selfish, and the insecure all exhibit similar behavioral traits, although more often than not, and due to social circumstances, one of these traits is more likely to surface than the others. Often the spouse realizes this later in life when isolated with such an individual.

A narcissist goes to great lengths to hide his flaws, going to irrational lengths to do so, including lying a lot, because he lives in constant fear of being seen, a fear triggered by his own shame. Here we have the narcissist's cycle, which begins with shame, moves to anger, and ends with demeaning and even bullying others. And interestingly, what triggers shame in narcissists is love, precisely because they can't feel it, and it exposes them the most. When a narcissist feels loved or respected, their shame about who they are is revealed. This is why they act like killjoys, spoilsports, and buzzkills. The happiness of others makes them terribly uncomfortable. In fact, it took me years to understand why so many people hated me so much for no other reason than that I smiled. Smiling triggers the insecurities of a very self-centered and insecure person.

Another indirect way to make the narcissist angry is jealousy, because they have a competitive mindset and assume that what others have is related to what they don't have. The success of others triggers their shame. So they have to belittle the accomplishments of others, or worse, destroy their reputations through slander. This happened to me when I became popular among my students. One of the teachers somehow could not sleep at night and was constantly plotting ways to get me fired. Being better is simply not acceptable in a group where there is at least one very negative individual. This is why in communist and socialist societies, where the idea that having more is somehow evil and dangerous, people are extremely hostile to the success of some, and standing out is seen as antisocial behavior.

The contrast between American and European or even Asian societies is very obvious in this regard, because while American values promote standing out and even promoting oneself, European values are against all of that. In fact, the wealthiest European families are generally unknown, even though they run a large number of business brands with a significant impact on society. The target of the worse people among us is quite obvious, because it is the individual who stands out as more qualified. This is why so many famous entrepreneurs claim to have been bullied as children.

The worst thing for a narcissist is to be confronted by someone who is polite, respectful, kind, intelligent, and honest in front of everyone else, because it shines a strong light on the terrible nature of the narcissistic individual. This drives the narcissist crazy and obsessed with destroying that person. We often think that such behaviors are normal in society because we find them often, but there is nothing normal about them, precisely because they are designed to distort reality in favor of the narcissist. Here we have the co-worker who slanders the reputation of someone who is simply doing his job well and is admired and respected by many; we also have the girlfriend or boyfriend who destroys your reputation among your friends and relatives because they love and respect you; we even see these things in areas where personal quality should be more important than rivalry, such as music, painting, and other art forms, where the artist is attacked simply because he is famous. Then we find the hatred of those who are wealthy, while those who hate have no idea how hard these individuals have worked to achieve such a lifestyle, and the haters themselves are often found among the laziest members of society.

Racism and xenophobia are also traits of shame and insecurity, which is why we often see them in nations that have built themselves by plundering other nations. You will see hatred of other cultures and peoples more often in those who are ashamed of their own past. We see a lot of racism and xenophobia among the British, for example, because they were the ones who did the most to oppress, steal and destroy other nations. Their hatred of Indians and South Africans because of the color of their skin can be compared to the enormous shame they feel for stealing trillions of dollars from the nations of these immigrants, who are then forced to emigrate to British territory in search of a better life.

Chapter 5 - The Roots of Racism and Xenophobia

Immigrants trigger the shame of the local racists, who then have to cover it up with chauvinism. We see something similar among North Americans who use their patriotism to justify hating immigrants, even though their nation is essentially made up of the descendants of immigrants who stole the land from the natives who lived there before the colonizers arrived. The shame of North Americans comes precisely from this lack of identity, since they have nowhere to go that they can call their land. A similar behavior can be seen among Israelis, and for the same reasons, because they have to justify their shame with racism against others who are much more Israelite than those who are stealing their land.

On a larger scale, we see that many of the world's problems simply distract us from the root cause of their existence. Many conflicts, from the political to the personal, arise from a lack of ability to see life through the eyes of others, to think like them and understand them. This is a mental handicap, not just a common trait. It gets worse when our view of life is filtered through only one lens.

An evolved person is then one who understands why some people want to know and understand more, thus fostering a sense of empathy for the struggles of others, while a less evolved person will be so terribly insecure that they will want to segregate themselves into a group that opposes another group. We see such behavior in sports, national pride, racist groups, and other forms of delusional pride in nonsense for which many often lose their entire lives. Those who see themselves as separate from others have a sense of competitiveness that they try to cultivate through every kind of seemingly positive activity, including reading books. We see them all the time, for these are the ones who consider themselves superior to others because of their choice of books.

Some of these people are so obsessed with themselves that they try to sell me books written by other authors they follow instead of asking me what kind of books I write or even making the effort to read them and compare the information. But this pre-selection of books, people, and information in general is exactly what makes them ignorant. The very thing they try hardest to avoid while claiming others are ignorant is what they end up embodying with their behavior.

Associated with these traits is the act of asking questions. My brightest students would ask and learn, while the dumbest would assume and judge. More than 10 years later in life, the differences between the two groups couldn't be more obvious, with the losing team failing terribly in life, with long hours, jobs they hated, and low salaries, and the winning team loving their work and their lives. The irony here is that I never saw any correlation between college grades and the outcomes students achieved later in life.

Those outcomes were always correlated with their attitudes. They regret when it is too late to make a significant change and the cost of past decisions is too high to allow any significant space or time for such change, which once was in the distance of a question never asked or an hour of distraction in which the student could have heard the answer I offered to someone and chose not to.

Often people go through life with their hands in their ears and their eyes down, completely ignoring the opportunities that come their way. It could even be a teacher answering a question for the colleague sitting behind them that they need to ask themselves. They have chosen to ignore that opportunity, and their choice has cost them their destiny. Everything in life is a result of the choices we make to listen or not to listen, and more importantly, who we follow. Fools often tend to empathize with other fools. It takes a special mind to recognize the value of information. One of the qualities such minds possess is humility.

I have never seen anyone as superior or inferior to me, and that is perhaps one of the most distinguishing characteristics of my personality that has brought me from the bottom to where I am now. I have always analyzed things from a higher perspective, which means asking questions and trying to understand the point of view of others. Sure, I have been deceived many times because people lie and I was naive enough to consider their point of view. But even those who lie teach you valuable lessons about self-love and self-respect. Without them, we wouldn't suffer, and without the suffering they cause, we wouldn't work so hard for a better life. We would settle for less, or whatever was good enough for us at the time.

Chapter 6 - How Fear and Conformity Enslave Us

Most people do not develop the necessary qualities that make them targets for the lowest among us, so for the vast majority of people, life is easy and boils down to doing what they see others doing. They read the books everyone tells them to read and think what the majority tells them to think. Their idea of right and wrong is whatever makes them seem socially acceptable to the majority. They are too afraid to be different, even though they all claim to be different.

It's actually a very strange aspect of society that people consider themselves independent when they don't have the ability to think independently or even the tools to learn how to do so. Worse, they don't have the conscience that their thoughts are not independent because they never reflect on them or try to change them for any reason. Instead, they rationalize that whatever proves them wrong is wrong, and then go back to whatever they were doing. The fact that some of them read more hasn't made them better in any way, and there is nothing in their experience that would justify believing anything they say or recommend. They see the world from the bottom of the evolutionary scale. To them, I am the fool for disagreeing with them and not wanting to read the books they recommend to me. To them, I'm just lucky, even though it's obvious that the books they've read have produced zero results in their lives, books they couldn't even explain properly because the author was probably complicating something that was already uninteresting and useless.

It is a curious aspect of such people that they would rather hate me for writing books that contradict their worldview than want to learn more and face their own mistakes, fears, and insecurities. But this is also the most devastating effect of the mind on an individual, when it acts as a tyrant, preventing them from seeing reality as it is, and instead keeping them enslaved in old thought patterns that don't allow them to see more.

I am not necessarily proud of reading a lot of books, but of being very quick to decide what to read and what not to read, and of having a critical attitude towards the information contained in the book, rather than being a blind follower of some popular figure. What motivated me to become a writer was precisely the realization that most books are garbage and most authors are entitled narcissists who have nothing to say and in some cases spread even more confusion. Interestingly, the same ability to see this is what makes so many people now call me arrogant and narcissistic. It is very interesting that once you see the world as it is, the blind hate you for seeing what they cannot see.

I have never seen so much stupidity in my life as when I start telling people that I write books for a living and they realize that my books don't fit into their selfish and childish world view. Their insecurities and fears come to the surface in a very ugly way, especially among those who claim to be Christians. It is amazing how much hell is hidden under the masks of those who want to appear holy and go to great lengths to appear good. The more I learned and wrote, the more the hatred of others increased, as if I had become a threat to their existence. This is because they are nothing more than a number in the system and terribly dependent on it to validate themselves. But personally, I don't compare my thoughts to what others believe in terms of quantity or quality, but in terms of efficiency, and efficiency can be learned, so it's nothing to be envied or ashamed of. In fact, it is wise to copy what has efficiently produced positive results in someone else's life. This is why whenever someone asks me for advice on writing a book, I tell them to write an autobiography. At least you can contribute to the enlightenment of the world with your mistakes, if not your successes.

Knowing what not to do and why is just as important as knowing what to do. So many of us fail in life, as others have failed, because of our ego and ignorance. Nothing does more to eliminate such self-inflicted suffering than books on personal failure. And yet people are too self-centered and insecure to write them. This is the paradox of human stupidity, that people reincarnate many times on this earth, repeating the exact same mistakes for the exact same reasons, because no one does anything to prevent it. Everyone is too obsessed with their little miserable lives, trying to appear more important than they really are, to care about others. Except that if everyone is like that, then we are included in those others. The selfish mind cannot conceive of that.

Chapter 7 - The Evolution of Perception

At the top of the evolutionary path as a human being, you no longer see reality as right and wrong, but as interesting and uninteresting, or effective information and useless personal opinion. And how interesting it is when people get angry because you tell them their opinions are worthless. They really think their opinions have value for no particular reason. The vast majority of people are incapable of comparing the self to the whole and see themselves as separate entities, yet ironically seek validation from the whole. Thus, people cannot make this distinction between what is theirs and what is not, and assume that everything is theirs, especially when it is validated by the Whole.

This includes their thoughts, which are often a reflection of what they see everyone else thinking. They then assume that what is normal is what has been normalized, and anything outside of that spectrum is not normal, and so they learn to fear it, never question their own beliefs, and instead allow themselves to be conditioned by those same beliefs. If anyone tells them otherwise, they reject it. In fact, it took me years to understand why so many people avoided talking to me until I realized that they simply could not have a conversation with someone who challenged everything they believed to be true. The more you know, the more the fools who create their identity based on popular views will reject you because you cause them an identity crisis. Many people I've met have even told me they can't sleep or have nightmares because of the things I've told them. Nightmares are the mind's way of fighting itself when it is contradicted and emotionally challenged. A nightmare is an insecurity coming to the surface to be healed. Except it never is, because the individual is too afraid to face his insecurities. That is why he has nightmares.

An even more amazing result of this is when people deny not only the facts, but the reality that accompanies them. Many people I've met literally say that I'm not a real writer to them because I don't fit into anything they believe about writers. They are so immersed in stereotypes and social roles that they cannot understand that writing a book is not an activity related to social status, but to knowledge, and that knowledge is validated not by the space or the product in which it is presented, but by its effectiveness. In other words, they are unable to evaluate the information behind the social images. It is as if they have been stuck in a childlike view all their lives where everything has to fit into a box and the world is nothing more than objects in boxes. They have no concept of the fluidity of reality.

This is the same reason why people are fatalists and assume that everything is fixed at birth. It's even worse when doctors say that all diseases are genetic or that intelligence doesn't change. This lie is perpetuated throughout the world because people are too stupid to imagine a reality where things do change. This worldview would challenge everything they believe to be true and make them realize that they have been lied to by the world they trust. They cannot do that, so they choose to believe that nothing changes and you are nothing more than a copy of everyone else in the box where you belong. This is why people ask me where I was born and then spend hours talking about it as if it defines me as an individual and the information about my birthplace contains everything they need to know about me. This tells me two things: one is that they invalidate my entire existence and identity, and the other is that they see themselves in the same way.

I see exactly the same problem with those who tell me they want to write a book, because they always ask me questions about how to promote and sell, and I have never met one person out of many who ask these questions who has actually asked me what people want to read or how to write a good book. Everyone is obsessed with being a writer, not justifying being a writer. Everyone is desperate for validation, not value. People are mentally ill, and writing a book is not going to change that, but they think their accomplishments will allow them to gain the respect they need to feel they deserve the life they have wasted.

This idea comes from a selfish mindset where people think they can impose themselves on others, even if they write nonsense. Then you end up with a world where most books aren't worth reading and many readers read nonsense. In both cases they complement each other at the lower end of the evolutionary scale, because one writes to feel important, the other reads to feel important. It takes a much more evolved soul to write books worth reading, and a more evolved reader to recognize such books. That's why I say I couldn't exist without my readers, we're both part of the same system, and I wouldn't be surprised if, by understanding my own writing, they wrote books I would want to read.

Chapter 8 - How Collective Ignorance Shapes Our World

An idea is only valuable if the majority values it, so we have the world we consider relevant because we make everything else irrelevant. You can apply this formula to anything, including technology, engineering, and business. As many inventors have discovered, a good invention in a world of idiots does not generate profits because the idiots do not see the value of what is being offered to them. This is easy to understand if you can imagine going back in time and bringing a television to a society that had to hunt to survive because this entertainment would distract them long enough to end up dead. There would come a point where they would realize that television was actually an addiction that was compromising their ability to survive as a tribe. Today, television plays a very different role because people see it as a way to escape reality and relax their brains. Without television, most people would probably go crazy thinking about their own existence.

A philosopher cannot have many friends for this very reason, and philosophers are misunderstood as people who waste their time thinking about nonsense, because the majority of society doesn't know how to think, doesn't see the value in thinking, and doesn't like to think. Once you learn how to think and begin to think effectively, you become aware of your own misery, which is exactly the opposite of what people want when they distract themselves with the company of others and the many forms of entertainment.

I remember once a teacher gave me the result of my national examination in philosophy and said, "We don't know how you did it, but you got the highest grade in the whole country". She was referring to the many philosophy teachers who were amazed at my score. They were amazed because they could not understand how a teenager could memorize so much complexity and explain it so well on an exam. But I was not surprised at my score because I could understand what those philosophers were saying, and I found the questions on the exam too easy for the amount of information I could convey. In fact, I wrote much more than I should have, precisely because I could see the application of everything these philosophers were explaining. However, I did not realize at the time that philosophy teachers could not see as much as I could, and I just thought of them as bad teachers who tended to complicate simple things.

These teachers were trying to evaluate in the same way they saw themselves, as regurgitating information they could not assimilate. And yet here we have a society of fools who think they can judge others for no other reason than their social position. Where else do we see this? Everywhere! Even the idiots at the airport think they can stop me from entering and leaving a country for no other reason than their position. They often don't know, don't understand, and don't care about the real purpose of their position. They see themselves as valuable because of their power to restrict others. But what other answer can I give to someone who asks, "How long do you plan to stay in this country?" As if the correct answer is not "as long as the law allows me"?

The last time I entered Thailand, I was told that two months was a long time to stay in the country, to which I replied, "That is what your law says I am entitled to". He then asked why I hadn't booked a hotel for 2 months, to which I replied, "Because I don't know yet if you're going to let me through". Simple answers that these idiots don't understand because they don't know how to do their job. It is the same problem all over the world. People have confused their authority with the purpose of their job because they do not know what they are doing. They are just playing a role without any real meaning. This is even more obvious with baggage handlers, who are constantly breaking travelers' luggage. I have never been through the Greek airport without a new suitcase being completely broken. This tells you a lot about the mental state of such people.

Interestingly, when people can't deal with life, precisely because they can't deal with all the incongruities in the realities they face, they have to conceptualize imaginary explanations for their existence and then continue to justify what happens to them, instead of realizing that the problems they attract are caused by their own choices. This is certainly the case with the many Greeks, Portuguese and Spaniards who deserve to be punched in the face, but think that being rude to others whom they deem inferior for no other reason than the color of their skin justifies their lack of professionalism and lack of civility. But what is even more interesting about the lies people accept is how far they can go in contradicting themselves without realizing it.

Chapter 9 - The Spiral of Avoidance

People often say that money isn't important, but they live in fear of losing their jobs and spend eight hours a day doing something they don't like in order to get a paycheck. They also say that their friends and family are the most important people in their lives, but they spend an entire week working with strangers. People say that happiness comes from within, but they always think about traveling somewhere else. People say that good food and weather are important, but they often want to live in colder areas if they can get a better salary. People say that good health is very important, but they constantly eat for pleasure, even when what they eat destroys their health. This hypocrisy extends to what they tell others to think and do because it is what they want to see them do and not what they would really do for themselves. For example, those who tell me that I should stay in one place and not travel everywhere cannot go anywhere themselves. So what I do must be bad because they cannot have it. It is the mediocre realization of a childlike adult.

Although sadness and depression are normal emotional states, as is happiness, there's a reason that negative states are more common, and it's because of the delusional paradigms that lead so many people into their own confusions about themselves and life. The more someone attributes the answers to their problems and emotions to something outside of themselves and their own choices, and the more they rationalize the causes as justified, the more they contradict themselves and the faster they spiral downward in their mental state. This kind of thinking is exactly what keeps people at the bottom of the evolutionary scale and why they can't get out of their situation.

Many think they can get out of their problems with more money, but that's not true, because the way they think will bring them back to where they are, precisely because they have learned to identify with the way they think. To prove yourself wrong is to accept that an entire existence has been wasted on being wrong, and that creates guilt and shame, which is why people can't deal with introspection. The more you fail in life, the less you want to introspect your own behavior. You can't make a person who is obsessed with escaping his own life think about his behavior, which is why teenagers usually don't listen to anyone telling them that drugs are harmful to their brains and bodies.

It is said that one must be humble to find the truth, but this humility has nothing to do with how we treat others, but how we see ourselves. We must be able to recognize our shame and guilt before we can take responsibility for our lives. It helps if you can trust a higher power, God, to guide you, and you see that God as your ultimate goal instead of yourself, because there is no limit to what you consider your true self. These are really the only two choices you have, because either you are aligned with a higher intelligence, or you are subject to the belief system of the collective and always act as a pawn in that game.

It may seem easier to give up personal control over our destiny, but there are many more risks involved. People may have different backgrounds and personalities and therefore respond differently to their challenges in life, but everyone processes information in the same way and will filter reality according to the same laws of the mind, so we can't say that there is subjectivity except in what concerns our personal choices. The higher levels of recognition include love as an emotion that fulfills us, as when we move towards the things that make us happy and when we contribute to the development of the planet, which is why loneliness is not natural for a human being. The only way a person could feel good about being alone would be if they were aware that the things they produce in moments of loneliness are communicating with others around them and creating important changes that require such sacrifice. This is why we see this attitude more often in artists and leaders.

Many people today may not realize that they are lonely, but the lack of physical contact, the lack of face-to-face interactions, and the constant use of social media for every kind of communication shows us that people are indeed lonely. The many distractions we have today don't change that fact. When you are next to someone, there is much more than words being exchanged, there are also emotions, perceptions, and a certain amount of nonverbal communication, and overall, these multilevel interactions help us understand more of what it means to be human.

Chapter 10 - Mental Enslavement in a Controlled System

One of the most important things about being human that people seem to forget because of the constant interaction in the virtual world is appreciation. People are now too obsessed with themselves and their needs and tend to forget the importance of recognizing the value of another human being. This is easy to understand when you interact with a child compared to most adults, because the child expects you to at least smile, answer their questions, and say goodbye when you leave. This is not the case with adults, who often can't even look you in the eye. A child is also more receptive to receiving gifts than adults. The child will smile when you offer her something, while the adult will begin to wonder about your intentions.

These differences in behavior have many causes, and we can even say that the child is naive, but the truth is that the adult has learned to internalize his thoughts and distrust other people. And while this behavior is to be expected, it can't be considered normal. Adults take too long to trust, and this makes interactions difficult, which is why so many people live lonely existences. But ignorance of these facts makes people even more isolated than they should be, at least in many cultures of the modernized world. As a result of spending more hours interacting with algorithms and less with people, the masses become even more obsessed with their own beliefs, simply because the virtual world is constantly replicating what they like to do in order to demand more of their interaction and attention.

If we reverse this paradigm to see how the individual changes through interaction with others, we see that the difficulty of change then comes as a crystallization of what already is-their internalized beliefs about themselves, others, and the planet. The result of this state of mind is that more people act with arrogance while being foolish about the things they believe to be true. It is like saying that because you know your house, you know the rest of the world. People then assume that they are right because their results in life are always the same, instead of realizing that their results are predictable because their choices are always the same.

This has two advantages for the system: One is that people are easily brainwashed and controlled because they don't want to change the paradigm imprinted in their minds; the other benefit is that the individual becomes predictable. However, this predictability is beneficial to the system, but not to the individual, who then becomes a slave to his own mind. This mental enslavement is reflected in the way people perceive information. For example, I am often asked how I can easily make friends in any country, and the answer surprises those who ask the question. Because people are too obsessed with their own view of the world, they never notice that the only way to make new friends is to do something different from what they see others doing. The simple answer is to create chaos. You must create chaos in the reality of others in order for behavioral change to occur. This means starting conversations with strangers, organizing your own events, and exploring new ways of thinking that align with the tendencies you observe.

Of course, people may be offended by your behavior and confused by your attempts to talk to them, but that is part of the process, and not everyone will react the same way. Then, by comparing the different reactions, you can reformulate a better strategy and adapt to it. But what happens with most people is that they believe something that is not true, and then they make it part of their personality. And when it doesn't work, they make up a reason why it doesn't work. It's called rationalizing observations that may or may not be true. In many cases, people are satisfied with having an answer, even if their answer doesn't solve anything.

This reminds me of an incident with a former friend. Every guy in our group of friends was interested in her and constantly paying attention to her, especially one guy who always insulted me with bad jokes and drove her to and from her house. I actually thought they were a couple when I first met them, and only later did I realize that the nonverbal communication she was giving me showed me that they weren't a couple and she wasn't interested in him. This guy had absolutely no advantage, even though he really believed that being next to her and driving her around town in his car would lead to something. Then she started showing signs that she was interested in me while everyone else in the group was completely blind to what was happening. Things developed between us, but when the rest of the group saw us together, they were shocked, and some even said: "How did this happen when you barely spoke to each other?" Basically what was happening was that I was reading the nonverbal communication and the nonverbal communication was giving me a lot more information than what people were saying or seeing.

Chapter 11 - The Unimportance of What People Say

What people say is often a lie or completely irrelevant. People talk to make themselves feel important, not because they have anything to say. They are more likely to express insecurities and needs in the way they speak than to say anything worth responding to. And even if you do respond to what they say, they're often so obsessed with themselves that they won't pay attention to what you say unless they can use it to make themselves look more relevant in a conversation. Then comes the mocking of others. It's an infantile way for insecure people to feel validated in a group, and it often has more to do with what they feel than what they can see.

Most people don't really see anything, they can only make assumptions, people don't know anything, but they assume a lot. Everyone has an opinion about things they know nothing about, and to my surprise, many people who have never written a book in their lives, who have never worked for a publishing company, want to give me advice on how to write books, and even get offended when I dismiss what they say as absolute nonsense. They think that what they believe based on popular opinion is more true than my own life experience or the money I make from what I know.

Whenever you are willing to step out of your comfort zone, you will inevitably be confronted by idiots who will furiously defend their right to never do so. "You are wrong because everyone here agrees with me" is probably the stupidest thing I have ever heard someone say, and yet she was over 70 years old, proving that people can be stupid for an entire lifetime and never learn anything that justifies their existence on this planet. Once you see people for what they are and not what they tell you, you see a lot more behind their masks, and then they really hate you. Why wouldn't they? You bring their insecurities to the surface. But the truth is that their very existence is an insult to everyone else because they mean nothing. They are nothing but false replicas of what they admire and want to emulate, not real people. They have no identity of their own. Often they cannot even explain their own feelings. This is because most of their emotions are triggered by unconscious beliefs and insecurities, not by rational events in their lives that justify them.

Watching Europeans stare at me in horror as I sip an espresso makes as much sense as trying to explain it to other Europeans who refuse to believe me. You go crazy talking about crazy behavior in a world that the crazy think is normal. When you show it, people fabricate new illusions to deny what their eyes show them. They cannot see anything with their limited consciousness. People are so stupid that you can repeat the same sentence several times and they will still do what they want to do, which is why it is often a total waste of time to try to explain something to someone who is just too stupid. I can repeat twice that the person next to me is not "Thai", but if the person I am talking to thinks she is, she will try to speak to her in Thai to confirm her opinion. It is the same when Turks or Serbs insist on speaking to me in their native language after I tell them I cannot understand them. Many people on this planet are just too stupid. That is why we need robots, not to replace them, but to have some basic common sense and intelligence in a world where there is none and most people are nothing but malfunctioning automatons insisting on false data.

Humans are useless for the simplest jobs because they are too stupid. The majority are mentally retarded and have no right to any job, not even serving coffee. Because, as I have often seen, they can't even remember a simple order, and worse, they can't admit that they made a mistake. In countries like Lithuania and North Macedonia, people are so stupid that you can say anything and they will bring something else. In Lithuania, the cakes I ordered often came with hair on top because they didn't care. I wonder how mentally ill a person must be to put a cake with a hair on it on a plate and give it to a customer like that. It is unbelievable. Lithuanians are unbelievably crazy. But it is impossible to say these things to people who live in their own mental worlds, because not only can they not see it, they interpret it as an attack on their country. When I tell my Chinese students that their country has terrible air, they tell me that only foreigners suffer from it, as if their delusional communist brains are adapted to breathing toxic levels of pollution and their people are not dying of cancer. It is hard to understand the stupid when they are fighting you for their right to die stupid.

Chapter 12 - How Perception Shapes Our Lives

Those who can't see much will always be surprised at what those who can achieve with their efforts can achieve, because they really have no idea how life works. Most people are so incredibly stupid that they constantly create their own karma on a daily basis and are unable to see it. They can only see reactions to their behavior, never what they are doing as wrong because they are unable to empathize or see things from different angles. The Polish are a perfect example of this retarded mindset. I have never seen people as rude and incredibly stupid as the Poles.

On the other hand, your life must be disruptive and offensive to others if you ever want to have one. Those who break preconceived notions always make enemies, first among the people they know and then among strangers they have never met. And unless you can create chaos in their reality, you will simply end up conforming to their expectations. Fear of what others think is the fastest shortcut to never becoming someone worthy of consideration and never achieving any dream. Aligning yourself with other people's expectations is the last thing you should want, because it will always make you unhappy. You can do more for yourself by creating dissent. In fact, you will never have disagreements with those who are not determined to stop you because they themselves are aligned with their own needs and are not running away from their responsibilities.

When there is no disagreement, people rationalize what they observe to make sense of their lives, and that's when they conceptualize that you must have a trick to get the results you can't get, or that you can somehow manipulate others to do the things you want them to do. Anything outside their comfort zone is always some great magical mystery, or at best a scam. Most people cannot see how their view of others reflects back to them as results in their own lives.

People's stubbornness also applies to finding a job. As I've seen many times, people refuse to believe anything that others disagree with, even if it may jeopardize their own future. When I tried to explain to my students how they should behave in order to find a job, they ignored what I said. I even tried to tell them that I had run many businesses before working as a university lecturer, but they probably thought I was lying. Their other teachers had zero experience in anything we can think of, even less experience than I had in teaching. So when we talk about insight, we are obviously also talking about effectiveness and pragmatism, which means that if people do not see the obvious, they are not only stupid, they are incompetent to survive. If people don't know that a piece of advice will increase their own chances of survival, with a better job and a better income, they're just not smart enough to survive.

And unfortunately, because the system is designed to make people feel like they're part of a structure controlled by others, it also leads them to this retardation, which is why chaos is necessary for evolution to occur, even if it's forced by financial collapses and wars.

Another problem of the mentally retarded is that since they can't see the difference between a belief and a fact, they insist on their beliefs to protect their self-esteem, because they think their self-esteem is more important than their survival. This is another consequence of the sheep mentality that a hierarchical system creates.

For a while I thought that the way people think or their reasons might have different causes depending on their cultural background, but then I came to the conclusion that it is based on the same principles. In fact, at the bottom of the evolutionary scale, people think the same way. Differentiation comes later, when people learn to think independently. Until then, people are emotional in their decisions, not rational, so if you give them what they want from you - that is, their emotional needs are met - they are more likely to accept whatever you tell them. The more infantile they are, which is the same as saying the more retarded they are, the more likely they are to accept any advice based on emotional attachments.

The result of a retarded society is then a dysfunctional society, because in such an environment people treat customers badly because they are not happy, they complain about irrelevant things because they are not happy, and they work as little as possible because they are not happy. When they vote, when they make any important decision, they will vote for those who promise them more happiness, even if what those leaders say is completely illogical and even dangerous.

Chapter 13 - Decision Making and the Illusion of Logic

Important decisions related to voting for who should be in power, as well as decisions made in job interviews, are motivated by the need to satisfy emotional needs. I tried to explain this to my students, but they were too obsessed with their own emotional attachments to recognize when someone was trying to help them, and later in life found themselves in jobs they hated while telling me they wished they had my life. This cycle repeats itself everywhere and for many generations. This is why I thought teaching was a complete waste of time. People are too stupid to be taught.

Although I initially believed that college students would be more independent and capable, it is the opposite - they are the worst - because they are already completely indoctrinated in the ways of society. They are perfectly adapted to a world that does not exist, so it is not surprising that so many college graduates end up unemployed.

One of the most time-wasting classes I ever taught was in Lithuania. I offered a class of students everything I knew about success in life, principles that took me a lifetime to learn, and they completely ignored it. Many of them were probably too focused on my appearance and skin color to care, because they seemed too racist and stupid to listen to a word of what I was explaining. Just like them, most people on this planet are completely worthless. Their eyes see nothing and their ears hear nothing. The only ray of hope for humanity is in the children, but if the parents prevent them from learning more effectively and call them stupid for asking the right questions, then any effort is demonstrably lost.

In addition, parents often disapprove of teachers who try to educate their children more effectively because they disagree with the methods, and in doing so these parents undermine their own children's future with what they think is right and replicate an already dysfunctional system. Instead of making their children better adults, they make them as worthless as themselves with their own beliefs.

Our emotions have a reason to exist, but they are not the most important aspect of making effective decisions, and we are often driven by fear and trauma when we use our emotions anyway. But because people are fundamentally driven by their emotions, and because their emotions are based on the irrational aspects of their minds, or in other words, experiences they have forgotten but which still affect their mental process and ability to make congruent and logical decisions, they filter their entire reality based on these irrational aspects of themselves. Many of the beliefs that people have make absolutely no sense, but they can't see that even when you show them, and that's the meaning of being unconscious.

You see these things everywhere, in politics, in education, in religion, in every aspect of society. It is this: "I'm doing it this way because everyone else agrees that this is the way to do it." And while we can't ignore the fact that how we respond emotionally affects how we are perceived, which means we have to create empathic communication to be understood, it's hard to empathize with the morons among us. They are completely unaware of their own lack of awareness, yet they insist that you are the problem, not them.

An example of this was a situation in Greece where someone kept making mistakes with my ferry ticket and yet told me that I was the problem, even though the messages clearly showed that she hadn't read anything properly. I have seen the same thing in many other countries, where people assume a lot about what they read, but cannot even look at the words. That is how far they are from reality. They cannot face the words, they assume things that are not written.

We all know people who assume things we never said because that is how their brains fabricate a reality, as if others are nothing but objects in that mental movie. The lower someone is on the spectrum of consciousness, the more likely they are to make assumptions. This is why the mentally ill always perceive threats where there are none, like when British ladies clutch their wallets when I am near them, or run away from me when I am walking, as if I were a threat to their existence. Many people are mentally ill beyond any logical understanding.

For these reasons, when we talk about empathic communication and feeling empathy for another person, we should be aware that these attitudes are not to be applied equally in every given scenario. The average mentally ill person will see these qualities as threats, and a psychopath will see these qualities as weaknesses to be exploited. As the psychopath knows, everyone has emotional buttons that can be pushed, and if a person is more empathetic, he knows that person is more likely to agree with whatever is being said, including a lie. Politicians do this all the time to get votes. If you do the same thing in a job interview, you will get the job even if you have no qualifications to get it, which is why psychopaths have no problem getting jobs and are often found in management positions. The human resources department in particular is often filled with psychopaths. This is where a company's problems with its employees begin.

Chapter 14 - Working for a Better World

If you are a very rational person, you will find yourself at odds with a world that refuses to think and will even tell you that you think too much. Emotional people do not care about reason because they are driven by emotion - the need for pleasure and the avoidance of pain, or the need for comfort and the avoidance of discomfort. They may hate you for no other reason than your skin color makes them uncomfortable, as has happened to me all over Europe. Not only that, but if you don't smile at people and try to empathize with them or respond to certain social buttons, people will simply hate you, even if you have done nothing to justify that behavior. If you don't believe me, try walking through society, talking normally, but never empathizing with anyone, never smiling, never talking about common interests, and you will see it.

This proves to us that people are still largely in their animal state, not in the human state of the evolutionary path. They do not use rationality except for the assimilation of threats in their environment, which are largely perceived through their delusional senses. The idea that we need to show emotion in order to empathize is not a sign of evolution, but the opposite - a demonstration of a lack of sufficiently developed intellectual qualities. The fact that we need to demonstrate that we are not a threat to those who perceive us as such has nothing to do with civility, but everything to do with succumbing to the pressure of a mentally ill person. This is very obvious when someone claims that I am experiencing racism because of the type of colors I wear. It is ridiculous to justify the behavior of the mentally ill and allow it to be perceived as normal. The need for people to see things as normal when they are not perpetuates the abnormality of the world.

The reason scientists label such things as normal human behavior is as relevant as their association of normal human behavior with the behavior of rats, which they systematically analyze in order to understand humans. But science, and psychology in particular, is only concerned with theories made from the observable, because that's where the money is, and scientists work for money, not for free. Thus, the study of deeper meanings is irrelevant to them and relegated to the realm of philosophy or religion. They equate what they can't measure not with their own ignorance, but with the realm of cultural belief.

Science, however, is just one of the many ways that people apply their own beliefs, which is why evolution seems so slow and difficult, especially to those on the front lines trying to push everyone else toward a better world. There is no interest in such a better world because there isn't even a belief that it is possible, or even a consistent effort to make such a possibility relevant. People are too preoccupied with their petty lives and their need for reputation and validation to care about a world they may never see get better. A world where efforts to change are met with resistance from the people who can benefit from those changes, not to mention those who will suffer from them. It doesn't matter how hard you work, how innovative and creative you are, because the rest of the world will always try to stop you, slow you down, push you backwards, or literally try to kill you if you push everyone too hard and they feel threatened, which is why so many holistic doctors with cures for extremely profitable diseases end up dying in apparent suicides.

The assassination of many important figures in our history also happened because they pushed too hard. They were called too greedy, too cynical, too controversial. These are words that society uses when it's bothered by people who think too much. In fact, when you know much more than anyone else, more than all the idiots who know nothing and have their heads filled with air, you are told to think less, to slow down, to relax more. This is what people tell me all the time, not because I think too much, but because they are too stupid, they do not think and they cannot understand what I am telling them. My thinking bothers them. The fact that I read much more than they do irritates them because it exposes their absolute ignorance. But no one has ever told me that they don't understand what I say. What they usually say is that there's too much information for them to understand, or that they have to read too much when I write.

Many of these people are looking for shortcuts, answers to complex questions that do not require too much time for them to study and assimilate, or at best, answers that fit their own expectations. In other words, they shift the problem from themselves to other people, as if it is not they who are too stupid to solve their own problems, but me for not having simpler answers or answers that fit their expectations.

Chapter 15 - The Resistance to Change and Evolution

People have a programming in their brains, a primate mindset of following what is known rather than evolving, that keeps people from ever changing. The truth is, you can judge a person by his environment because he quickly learns to conform to it. In fact, a U.S. Travel Association survey found that about 40% of Americans have never traveled internationally. An Ipsos Reid survey found the same figure in Canada, that about 40% of Canadians have never traveled internationally. According to a survey by the Foreign & Commonwealth Office, about 35% of British adults have never been abroad. What's more, it's estimated that about 50% of people in the UK live within 20 miles of where they were born. If these are the numbers for some of the wealthiest nations, we can easily estimate that most of the world's population knows absolutely nothing about the planet they live on.

According to the United Nations World Tourism Organization (UNWTO), there were approximately 1.4 billion international tourist arrivals worldwide in 2018. However, this number represents only a fraction of the world's population, indicating that a significant portion of people have never traveled internationally. Most people still live like medieval peasants. They know almost nothing except what they are allowed to know. Yet many don't read, don't educate themselves, and ridicule those who do. This makes no sense. It is like being ridiculed for evolving by a bunch of monkeys who decide to live in the same tree and eat bananas forever.

The truth is, the dumber someone is, the more they expect an answer to be simple because they expect their own world to be simpler. They do not want inconvenience, they do not want to change, and they will fight for their right not to change. Wars are all about not wanting to change, otherwise you would know that you can just pack up and move somewhere else and start over. In fact, it is ridiculous to miss a country that had nothing to offer before a war broke out and was going nowhere anyway. If you are a businessman, a writer, a painter, or even a musician, you should want to change with your work if you want to improve, because it is literally impossible to be significant as an individual while reducing yourself to the spectrum of visible reality around you. All the great thinkers valued complexity, and complexity comes from exploring what we do not know.

One of the most common mistakes people make is to assimilate everything they want into what they need, and so in their arrogance they believe that wealth must correspond to buying a big house where they were born, having an office to show other people, and going to places that others consider signs of social validation. I once met a woman who told me she wanted to visit the Maldives, yet she lived in the middle of Europe, a bus ride and a few hours away from several nations, and had never been to any of them. And why visit the Maldives and not the countries surrounding the same waters? Social validation! The same reason people want to write a book about nonsense.

Interestingly, because people often overcomplicate their assumptions based on their beliefs, they fail to see the simplest answers in front of them, either it's a book they will never read or consider reading, or an author they refuse to listen to because they don't like what he says and make them feel uncomfortable. But as I always say to those who have big dreams, everything happens one step at a time. It is simply not possible to compare my results as a writer to the average person, because I spent a lifetime preparing for this, even though I did not know it would be my career. Yet people who have no significant life experience, only a big ego to consider, can compare themselves to someone who has worked their whole life as a college lecturer, a business consultant, and an expert in pedagogy. How does that make sense?

People are so deluded and so incredibly arrogant that they think there is a shortcut to that amount of technique, knowledge, and life experience. And how do you distill thousands of books into a 5 minute conversation? People believe it is possible, so they insist on it, and then they say I talk too much when I answer them. Why would I talk too much unless I wasn't interested in giving them the answers they didn't want to hear based on the way I acted?

Attitude says everything about a person, and most people simply do not have the attitude of someone who is committed to their goals. Our attitude is a reflection of our thoughts, our thoughts control our decisions and actions, and the consistency of such thoughts and results determines a person's financial results and even health. If you don't like fruits and vegetables, you are setting yourself up for cavities, cancer, and Alzheimer's disease.

Chapter 16 - The Misalignment of Expectations

Money is a means of transaction, and as such it goes where the flow is greatest. That flow is determined by attention and social value, which is why toilet paper sells better than books. But to say that toilet paper is more important than books would be nonsense. That's why logic and popularity don't always coincide with true value, and value doesn't always reflect financial goals. You are more likely to get rich by solving problems that people want to solve than by writing books that nobody wants to read, even if such books provide the answers that people need.

This is why wealth does not correlate with spiritual enlightenment. When someone asks me how much money I make selling spiritual books, they are starting from the wrong perspective and showing me how ignorant they are about reality, money and spirituality. In fact, you won't reach many people with spiritual subjects unless they are predestined to learn them, and that means they have already reached a certain level of consciousness that makes them ready for such subjects. This is why the idea that when the student is ready, the master will appear is as valid for books as it is for therapy, because those who seek out a therapist have the decency to recognize that they have problems to solve, while those who are too insane to have self-awareness will never do such things. Just as those who don't read are the ones who need reading the most, those who think they don't need therapy are often the ones who need it the most.

The problem is that the choices people make lead to the world we all have to go through and experience and call reality. And so we are stuck with a society of largely incompetent and mindless people who act on instinct like wild animals. A society where everybody wants to pay for little papers that wipe their ass, but nobody wants paper that wipes their brains of the shit that's in it and stinks because they can't see how ugly and filthy they are. But the truth is that the racists, the nationalists, and the xenophobes probably slept through their history classes and need a tremendous amount of education. The rude, the chauvinists, and the narcissists need a lot of therapy because they know nothing about themselves. And the rest, who can't even be categorized, are so lost that they will probably have to go through death to learn anything useful, because they won't understand anything about spirituality even if they try.

When Buddha said over two thousand years ago that you must practice detachment through meditation to overcome pain, he was not saying that you must be apathetic to it, but rather that you must know yourself to know how you cause your own misery. This practice requires introspection, and meditation was the way people did it in ancient times. Today we have many more methods that allow this, but many still refuse to go through them. However, if more people were aware of how stupid they are, they would probably feel the need to read more.

This self-awareness, however, is something the very ignorant don't have, which is why they do nothing about it. Meanwhile, life as it is doesn't give them enough pressure to feel the need to learn and invest in their own education, even when they are absorbed by multiple pressures and suffering. As a result, they don't like to pay for books, but have no problem paying for bottles of water, often filled with the same water from their kitchen. They also claim to have no money for food, but spend what little they have on absolute garbage. In fact, people worry too much about the price of meat and not enough about the price of fruit because they eat none. This is perhaps one of the biggest signs that animals are at least smarter about their health. It takes a certain level of consciousness to realize the importance of these things, and many people are very lost. Yet they think that motivation will solve their problems, as if a madman with determination is better than a fool with none.

In this respect, the psychopath has an advantage because at least he recognizes that knowledge gives him an advantage over others. The problem with the psychopath is that he is not very good at consistency, and so he seeks shortcuts. The need for short answers is a psychopathic trend in our society, because only a healthy person will seek to understand more, not just get quick fixes to life and have an advantage over others. The more mentally ill someone is, the less able he is to assimilate different points of view, which is why he doesn't want to make the effort to empathize and understand different points of view, such as reading widely.

It is indeed logical that many entrepreneurs hire psychopaths to run their companies because they want to see higher profits in a shorter period of time. But it is also not surprising when these same psychopaths run the companies into the ground after helping them make profits. We think these things happen because of fluctuations in the market and the economy because we don't connect the two elements - the psychopaths and the fluctuations in the market. But the future of a business like a country can be accurately predicted based on the character of those who make the most important decisions.

Chapter 17 - The Isolation of the Developed

The biggest problem, often invisible to those who can think but don't understand this world, is that it is mostly run by psychopaths and retards. Those who are normal and live an organized and predictable existence are constantly confronted with jealousy hidden behind justifications that usually have no correlation to the facts. In such a world, people who are more compassionate, thoughtful, empathetic, and intelligent are perceived as weak, naive, and constantly pushed around by the rest of society as if they were inferior, ineffective, and even useless. The opposite is true, but you can't expect both psychopaths - who cannot manipulate and control such individuals - and the vast masses of mentally retarded - who value their emotions over results, even when those results affect their own survival - to see these things.

The only path left for those who are more evolved than the rest of the human species will be the same one they have faced for the past millions of years: to leave their tribe, which is another word for family and culture, experience loneliness, and start a new life with a family or alone.

The common point in all these stories is reciprocity, because a belief is only effective if it has reciprocity. If you have knowledge, beliefs, and an awareness of life that is advanced but not accepted, you don't have that reciprocity, no matter how right you may be, and that's what isolates you. This was the problem that great inventors like Nikola Tesla faced. In essence, Tesla wasn't good at empathic communication because he wasn't focused on it. His focus was much more evolved than that, as he looked to the future, not to the emotional needs of others. As a result, he died alone, in a hotel room, with only pigeons for friends, watching the world change before his eyes with his inventions and no recognition of his name. What a sad existence this was, but also very demonstrative of the kind of world we have. Tesla wasn't ignorant in any way, he was just too advanced for his time.

In a world of fools, the tyrants and dictators are more likely to get recognition and respect, which is why so many psychopaths have taken advantage of this mass stupidity to drive the world towards more ignorance, abuse and wars that have killed millions. The inventions of Nikola Tesla could have created a great revolution in the world, but they meant the end of profits for oil, gas and electricity. This would be a new world of equal opportunity, where the bankers who sponsored the new inventions would no longer increase their wealth, and no one would be able to make a business out of controlling the energy supply. Such a world would develop extremely quickly because we wouldn't have one or two nations dominating everyone else on the planet, but a whole planet contributing to the same progress. The masses wouldn't be so obsessed with meeting their basic needs for food and water, but would invest in their education and the progress of the planet.

In such a world, hierarchies could no longer exist because they would prove useless. So the psychopaths, in their greed, made sure that this world would never exist and have kept any glimpse of such a reality away from the common people ever since. You can't have wars unless people are too stupid to see why they're happening and who benefits from them, and that's usually the case. This has been the case in the past, and it is still the case today, as recent wars show us.

For example, people don't see that the United States funded and trained terrorist organizations like ISIS and other extremist groups to help in the capitalist war to overthrow governments that opposed the interests of North Americans and Europeans. When the United States then decided that it was more profitable to fund both sides of the conflicts, they decided to send their own soldiers to die because a human life became too cheap compared to the billions that could be made from the arms trade. The masses, brainwashed by what they read and see, think that there is a war on terrorism, when in fact what is happening is the complete destruction of the Middle East and the transformation of democratic nations into absolute tyrannies in favor of the ideals of the Europeans and North Americans. The poor and homeless victims of these wars then have to seek asylum in nations that treat them with absolute contempt and racism, while earning a salary, in many cases below the average of the people of those nations, just to keep themselves alive.

When Russia decided to defend itself against an imminent invasion from the United States through Ukraine, the masses once again chose to be stupid and demanded an end to this war, even though they never did so for any of the other 30+ wars that the United States and NATO combined have waged for absolutely no reason other than their own greed. As if that weren't enough, the masses proved once again how easily they can target and discriminate against a group of people when the psychopaths in power tell them to, by hating Russians for no other reason than their nationality.

Chapter 18 - The Silent Driver of Wars and Prejudice

We have wondered in the past how people turn against whole nations and groups of people, and then we saw how the whole world turned against Russians for no other reason than their nationality when Russia invaded Ukraine in 2022. Suddenly Russians could not withdraw money from their bank accounts because they were born in the wrong country. We saw the same thing when Gaza was invaded by Israel in 2023, and people saw the murder of thousands of children as justified for political reasons. As I have noticed when talking to people from different nations about the problems of the world and the many conflicts we still witness, they have absolutely no idea why things happen the way they do, and often bring their own emotions and personal needs into the conversation as if it were an argument to find logic in their beliefs.

North Americans and Brits do the same thing, which is why they don't protest wars in the Middle East where people of what they consider the wrong color and religion are dying. They protest wars in Ukraine because those people are more like what they can consider a normal human being - white and Christian. Racism is very much alive today because racism is a trait of the very stupid, and racism justifies many wars because it is driven by personal emotions often rooted in delusional self-image and absolute ignorance of history and science. Although people don't say it openly, the main reason why they approve of some wars and not others is always driven by their emotional worldview.

The same goes for people's choice of life partners, because they will have sex with people who look different from them for entertainment, but will only consider someone who looks like them to raise a family. As I've noticed, interracial couples are rare because people don't see love as a priority, but rather as the result of a combination of other elements that have failed in their lives. They will marry someone they haven't considered if the alternative is to be alone. Again, this is a decision made out of selfish desires, not love.

I don't expect many of these people to admit it, and there are certainly always exceptions, but there are advantages to having telepathic abilities that go beyond what many on this planet are willing to admit about themselves and their world. In fact, it is ridiculous to consider a heaven on earth unless you are willing to reveal your thoughts. The more you have to hide, the less you can be seen as a soul ready for a significant transition that doesn't mean coming back here and starting all over again. When you can read people for who they are, you become aware of how much they resist their own honesty. They do this because appearing to be a good person is more important to them than actually being a good person. This is why many people won't admit that they are racist, even though they constantly make racist comments and observations about everyone.

They remind me of a friend of mine who used to tell people that she was a vegetarian, even though she could not go a day without eating meat, and got angry when I actually decided to stop eating meat. If you are an ethical person, when the liars can't admit their lies, it is your duty to expose them for the liars they are, no matter how much they protest and call you a liar for exposing their lies. Moreover, it is expected and quite ironic that you will be accused of doing what the liars do, because that's how liars react when they are exposed.

There is no better context for judging people's behavior and values than when they are choosing a mate. It is in these moments that much about their true nature comes to the surface. In fact, the reason so many people think it's difficult to find a good life partner is because they don't think about this dynamic, or even how they apply their own delusions to their behavior. The truth is that both women and men look for a certain reciprocity when they are looking for a life partner, whether they are heterosexual or not, and regardless of their sexual interests, because there are even men who believe that they can marry a virtual woman and will die for her if she corresponds to what they need.

When we are dealing with humans, this reciprocity tends to be more complex and includes eye contact, non-verbal communication, smiles, and questions. It will take a long time for people to realize this, especially if they think artificial intelligence can replace their need for validation when they have delusions about themselves and don't even know themselves that well. Notice that an interested person will ask questions, and if someone is too quiet, that person is probably not listening. But there is a difference between being polite and being honest. An AI machine will not be so honest as to cause conflict. But that is what a good friend should do.

Chapter 19 - The Irrational Forces That Shape Our World

The need for reciprocity and social validation begins as soon as there is an awareness of certain aspects that correspond to personal interests or needs, but without self-awareness, reciprocity can lead to a greater delusion about oneself, which is what happens when people associate with those who tell them what they want to hear rather than the truth. For men, these needs tend to be associated with social validation as well as physical attraction, which is why they may be interested in a woman of poor character if she is well dressed and feminine enough. For women, validation is also associated with physical and social aspects, but in this case it is attributed not so much to gender as to income, and not so much to how a man presents himself as to his position in society-the amount of implicit or explicit power he has.

Implicit power can be related to social influence and finances, while explicit power is the actual possession of a position that automatically confers power. Women are automatically attracted to such men for obvious reasons that they may not even think about, although this is a biological drive that has been around for thousands of years. From a more primitive aspect of this reality, it is obvious that these men are more likely to dominate and overpower others. They are not necessarily the most empathetic, which is why women then claim to be abused in their relationships, even though such empathy was never a criterion in their choice of mate.

Men who are driven to positions of power and control tend to be psychopaths, but women can't see it that way, which is why many say that all men are the same. When I asked women who say all men are the same to describe such men to me, they described a very small percentage of society, they mentioned men I rarely meet, and men I wouldn't even consider working with or having as friends. In essence, most women are attracted to psychopaths because psychopaths are the ones who trigger the most attraction mechanisms in women. Consequently, most women reproduce with the lowest percentage of the masculine spectrum, and that is where psychopaths are found. The irony here is that the more insecure a woman feels, the more likely she is to be attracted to a dominant man, typically a psychopath, so when we talk about domestic violence or women being subservient to very possessive men, we are not really talking about inequality or a gender war, we are talking about a very specific problem.

Insecure women are attracted to possessive and dominant men, who in turn are more prone to violence and psychological abuse, precisely because they need to dominate others by force to feel validated. We then destroy an entire society because women are too emotional in their choices and choose the most violent men, and also because when they do choose, they choose men without any empathy. And when we claim that the world keeps repeating the same struggles, we fail to acknowledge that it is because people keep making the same choices and reproducing for the same reasons, perpetuating the same type of genes.

Not only that, but education in its various forms reinforces popular beliefs because popular beliefs sell. It is interesting to note, for example, how love stories, from those told to children to those promoted in adult romances, are always about men of power - princes, kings, and business owners - getting the most naive of women - hopeless, lonely, and full of dreams. Has the increasing independence of women changed this dynamic? What the statistics show us is that women are simply getting divorced more often and are more likely to end up alone, raising children by different men for exactly the same values and reasons. Not addressing these issues may make us more tolerable, but not judging what is happening based on the known data will not change the results.

In essence, whatever the issue, we see that the dynamics of the world have changed to fit people's emotional needs, not because they make sense. When people say that love is more important than reason, they are literally saying that irrational motives based on emotions rooted in delusional assumptions make more sense to them. People don't care about logic or reason because they will bend any rules and change any laws to suit their emotional needs. This is why there are so many laws for the most ridiculous scenarios. As society becomes more abnormal and mentally ill, the number of laws will increase, but not the order. The laws will simply chase the chaos that will continue to spread throughout the world. There is one way to organize society in a natural way, but many ways to experience chaos, and no end to the number of laws we can create to reinforce an order that will never be understood or accepted.

Chapter 20 - The Psychopathic Roots of War and Conflict

Those who can't live in this chaotic world are driven to isolation and extinction, which is why the suicide rate among middle-aged men continues to rise, up to four times that of women. No one cares about these men. Women certainly don't care because they have excluded them from their mate selection criteria, and psychopaths don't care about these men either because they have most likely abused them because psychopaths dominate by force and are greedy. The only hope for these men is within themselves, in their isolation, which is why so many men over 40 never marry or have children.

We come to another paradox that tells us that if you don't like society as it is, you still have to study and assimilate it if you want to survive, overcome mental illness, and be successful. You may never agree with what psychopaths think and do, but you still have to study them. You need to know how they see the world and what their plans are in order to find a way out of the chaos. It is also because we have psychopaths in this world that we cannot ignore violence. In a world full of psychopaths, conflicts arise in everyday life and will come to us if we simply demand to be respected, because psychopaths disrespect all the time. They see politeness as a weakness, so they themselves contribute to such a world.

In nations like Greece, Portugal, Spain, Poland and Lithuania there are so many psychopaths everywhere that you end up fighting for the simplest things just because the people of these nations are extremely disrespectful. Disrespect is so common in these places that they will tell you it is part of their culture. In their world, there is no such thing as agreements and peaceful coexistence. To them, you are either predator or prey. Psychopaths have a binary view of reality. Some of the things they say are actually very revealing of what is going on in their minds, such as, "If you agree with what I say, it is because you are too weak to have an opinion of your own". In other words, they cannot see agreements as two people thinking together to get the best result, but as one person dominating another with his own point of view. This is why you waste your time trying to explain logic to a psychopath. They don't care about logic, only dominance, and that dominance may come by force if they perceive you as too weak to hurt them or too polite to disagree, which is why agreeable personalities are more likely to suffer emotional abuse. For psychopaths, there is no such thing as common sense, facts, or logic, only winning and losing opinions.

This dominance is often used by psychopathic women in public because they know many other people are stupid enough to interfere in their defense, and it's also how they use other men against one who is often the victim of psychological abuse. By using other men's violence, a psychopathic woman can then use violence against her target. In some cases, psychopathic women will even use physical violence in front of other people, knowing that society will intervene against a man who reacts in his defense.

It is not uncommon, although this subject has not been studied enough, that many wars were not actually started by kings against kings, but rather by queens. In many cultures it is said that behind a strong man there is a strong woman, but this is a rationalization of a psychopathic trait in the world. It is more accurate to say that behind a very emotional, powerful and pleasant man, there is most certainly a psychopathic woman. These men are often controlled by psychopathic women, and both are attracted to each other for the reasons already mentioned, because a very reactive man is essentially a very emotional man. In a world dominated by psychopaths, it is only normal that most women feel insecure and therefore seek men who will make them feel secure.

Much is debated and researched about attraction, but we always come back to the same points: Women are interested in a well-dressed and strong man because he represents trustworthiness, social validation, and security; women also initiate conversations with men they perceive as having high social value because, again, these men have passed the validation test. It is said that women never approach men they are interested in, but this is said by women who are lying and by men who have never experienced power. Women have always approached me and given me their phone number when I was perceived to have high social value, namely when I was traveling, when I was speaking in public, when I was well dressed in a suit, and when I was simply popular with many people. In fact, when I lived in the United States, North

American women often approached me because of the way I was dressed. I met dozens of them in just a few weeks, and in every case they initiated the conversation, not me.

Chapter 21 - Personal Interests and the Future of the Planet

I have noticed a correlation between mate selection behavior and intelligence in both men and women. In the case of women, for example, when women are less intelligent, they perceive their need for security not in terms of a man's value to society, but in terms of their physical strength. This would be the same as a man going back in time and trying to flirt with a medieval woman working in the fields, as she will clearly be more interested in a man who knows how to use a sword and ride a horse than one who reads books. Reading books has no value in a world where dominance is determined by physical strength and the willingness to kill. In the poorest nations of Europe, these traits still prevail, as women tend to prefer men who are strong and tall, not more intelligent.

In essence, women seek security, which they find in monetary achievements, physical attributes, or mental qualities, but these things vary depending on where you are, which is why some men can be invisible in certain cultures and very attractive in others. If intelligence is an irrelevant characteristic, it is because such a culture is too primitive to value intelligence, and in primitive countries strength and appearance take precedence in social dynamics. That is why Lithuanians are extremely racist and xenophobic. People may not like those who expose or admit these truths, but that is because their emotions take precedence over self-reflection.

The masses do not like to analyze themselves because they are incapable of doing so. This is the same reason why many Lithuanians, who are themselves descendants of Russians, claim to hate Russians, or why Spaniards claim to dislike Arabs, but are themselves descendants of Arabs, or why Croats and Greeks are racist against Turks, even though they were literally part of Turkey during the Ottoman Empire and for almost a thousand years. These are the same people who hate each other, and yet the more primitive a civilization is, the more likely it is to avoid self-reflection about its own behavior and even its origins. Interactions are driven by instinct, based on irrational reactions rather than common sense.

There is no such thing as common sense in areas dominated by stupid people. But you can easily understand how people think and behave by organizing social events, which I have done many times and for many years in the more than thirty countries in which I have lived. Over time, you will see what types of people are attracted to social interactions and why, and what types of events they are most attracted to. As you continue to make these associations through observation, you will find that most people may not feel empathy for you, but those who do will become your new friends. In many cases, the reasons why someone wants to be your friend or not can be completely absurd and can change within minutes.

For example, Europeans, North Americans, and Brits are typically selfish and motivated by personal interests, so they may ignore a person they perceive as being of little value, and then start smiling at that person and inviting them to dinner when they want something from them. This was very obvious to me when they found out how much I traveled or that I was a writer. It doesn't happen as much with South Americans, Africans, and Asians because they are more interested in making friends based on conversations about topics that both parties are interested in talking about, which actually makes a lot more sense from a human perspective. This is why I tend to say that the future of the planet is not in Europe or North America, because you cannot develop a planet if people are only concerned with their own personal interests and are cruel to others and discriminate based on appearances and their own opinions or what others can offer them. This is a kind of slave and slave master mentality, between colonialists and colonized, that no longer makes sense, but is prevalent in many cultures.

If you can see these things, of course others will find you confusing, because they will not understand someone who disrupts their well-organized view of the world. If you call them out on their behavior, they'll think you're crazy because they don't see anything wrong with their behavior. If cultural traits are too intrinsic to a person's view of himself, he will not see it as wrong because it creates a conflict in his self-image. This is why racists get offended when you call them racists, even though they are racists acting on racist stereotypes. This is why people get punched, people get shot, and countries go to war.

That is why my perspective on war is very different from most people's. I've come to realize that conflict is inevitable, that racism cannot be defeated by reason, and that discrimination based on primitive aspects makes no sense if we are to evolve beyond a stage of mass schizophrenia, which is why war against the most destructive elements of society is always justified. The problem is to identify which elements these are and how to find them, and this is another challenge in this world, because often the target chosen and identified as the enemy is the wrong one. But that is what insanity and ignorance really are, targeting the wrong targets due to lack of wisdom, insight and mental clarity. When people are deeply insane, they murder the innocent.

Chapter 22 - Breaking Free from Cultural Norms and Evolving Consciousness

You are not evolved enough until you can distance yourself from your own position in society and then identify yourself as the enemy of the masses with the light of reason and progress. It takes a very evolved soul to be able to do an inner analysis and a separation of biology and spirit in the process of identifying problems. This is why I criticize Europeans so much, even though I am one, and even though I obviously do not compare my readers from Europe with the rest of the continent. This distinction is inevitable if we are to progress as human beings. It is also normal that at the highest levels of this progress you stop seeing the separation as coming from below - flags, territories and colors - and start seeing it from above - consciousness, evolution of perceptions and knowledge. Then, and only then, can you hope for a better world. Until that level is reached, our museums will be just another perspective of the same thing, related to the past but representing a parallel present.

The last thing society wants is chaos, because it disrupts the system of beliefs that everyone agrees on, but as the leader of your own life, you will always become a disruptive element of society - you will become unpredictable and as such considered dangerous. The reason people always sneak up on me when I write is because they think I am unpredictable. They do not understand me or what I am doing. They simply see a threat, and because they are driven by emotion and not reason, they try to find reasons to justify their own emotions. They are fundamentally insane, but they can't see it, and this is another problem you will face as a disruptive element in society. You will see that people are completely insane, always justifying irrational emotions and not being able to see it. Therefore, you will be forced to separate yourself from many people who will think you are cruel because they can't see that you are simply letting go of those who are already mentally dead.

The vast majority of the population is not alive, and your emotional attachment to them is an illusion, so when you suffer from disappointment and betrayal, you are actually suffering from your own delusions disintegrating in your mind. The more conscious you become, the more you realize how evil people are, because evil is correlated with unconsciousness, and with this realization you see that you are never dealing with real people, but with corpses motivated by a very low level of energy, guided at best by animal instincts. This realization doesn't make you a worse person, even though others will see it that way. It makes you more empathetic and realistic because you will be able to see which individuals are awakening, and with that ability you will be able to connect with the right people more quickly.

Once you become successful outside the mainstream, you become an undesirable person to those who depend on the system to survive, but also very admired by those who need more truth and honesty in their lives and see you as a light on their path. This is what it means to be enlightened. It is perceived for short periods of time and according to the contextualization of our attitude. This was certainly the case with the ancient philosophers of Greece, who were simply thinking about issues that most people of their time were ignoring and even rejecting. If you consider that many of them discussed happiness, you can see that it was a big problem for their people because they were unhappy. In many cases, such philosophers were expelled from their cities.

Nowadays, the most discussed topic is money, because people have found out that happiness isn't enough according to what those philosophers said, but only common sense. The Greek philosophers agreed that if you have enough food, a house, and a normal life, you should be happy, but now people don't see it that way. People now see these things as essential. They weren't essential before, they were rare, which is why we tend to see the things we devalue the most as important only when we don't have them. Our beliefs, needs, and values, like our cultures, are ephemeral, imaginary, and ridiculous to obsess over, which is why they can only be preserved in museums. As one evolves, one finds oneself isolated from the culture of one's birth, and that's a good thing, it's something we should desire, not avoid.

Unfortunately, many people have false beliefs about life and the choices they make. They rarely consider their beliefs to be wrong. To do so would imply that their personality is wrong. It is an attack on their ego that they don't want to take. It then becomes natural for them to justify their results by seeing guilt in others or some act of criminality in them. They do this because for them to be different is to be wrong, and to be wrong is to act against the law. You can see this parallel throughout history. For example, some people hate me because I know more than they do. Instead of assuming that they are too ignorant, they think that I get my information from some secret agency and that I should not know more than they do. In the not so distant past, many people who knew more were imprisoned, tortured, and murdered for no other reason than that they knew more than the masses. Now they are being discriminated against because of the same attitude of the past.

Chapter 23 - Cultural Toxicity and the Corruption of the Self

People's justifications and explanations may vary, but they don't evolve, which means they can make up a lot of explanations for things they don't understand, but they can't accept anything above their state of mind, much less see it as quite inferior to what would be desirable. This is obvious in many groups that consider themselves above everyone else, whether in politics or religion. The more people feel a conflict of interest with observable facts, the more they reject their observations and the less they look within themselves for answers, because those answers are often unpleasant.

It then happens that those who see the truth the most are pushed further away by the inability of others to accept anything that conflicts with their selfish views. In many of these groups, I'm actually called selfish, because if people can't get you to agree with them, they think you have an ego problem, not them. Isn't that interesting? People end up insulting you with their own problems because they are too stupid to listen to their own words and see who they are addressing.

The non-arrogant person listens and debates with facts because he's willing to change his mind when confronted with a higher truth. But the arrogant person cannot do that, and instead tries to drag that higher truth down with insults, delusional judgments that bear no resemblance to reality, and absurd justifications that ignore the most obvious facts and common sense. Because the arrogant is arrogant, he cannot see that he is arrogant. This is why many Masons and Rosicrucians, while seeking enlightenment, find more darkness instead. The more I traveled and interacted with many of them in different countries, the more I realized that they are some of the dumbest people I have ever met. I am not necessarily associating a group with a behavior here, but rather stating the fact that many people seeking enlightenment have found more darkness because they lack the ability to change themselves, and rituals certainly do not help them in any way. Following these patterns, many believe that value is somehow a secret that must be protected and not shared, so they ask many questions but answer nothing about themselves, never realizing their own limitations.

When you talk, when you do it honestly, you end up understanding more about yourself. To speak honestly is a sign of intelligence. It's the stupid who can't be honest because they see communication as a kind of battlefield. Poor nations in particular show this kind of thinking. They are so used to scarcity that they think happiness is a limited commodity, so if you smile more or show that you know more than they do, they see it as arrogance and abuse of power, as if you have no right to be yourself and proud or just happy with life. If you want to know the evolutionary level of a nation, you can use this criterion, because it quickly becomes obvious that Poland and Lithuania are among the least evolved nations in the world.

Following the same belief, many people hide their happiness, they hide what makes them proud, such as their relationships or their knowledge, because they don't want others to know that they are improving themselves. It's ridiculous, but very common in many people who are mentally ill and who live in sick nations and sick cultures that promote mental illness. Without realizing it, your need to fit in and have a pleasant existence leads you to conform to the ideals of those around you, and that is why, despite all the knowledge you accumulate, you are corrupted by the culture in which you find yourself, like a plant that feeds on poisonous water.

Many aspects attributed to a culture are nothing more than generalized tendencies, like when Filipinos assume that it is normal to be rude to foreigners, very slow, and extremely incompetent at their jobs. If you have a stomach ache because they sell you rotten food, they never see it as their problem, but yours. That is the culture. You can see that as people go down in their mental health, they become more and more self-centered.

The tendency toward self-centeredness is also the cause of a lot of loneliness in the world. But this effect is also present in many therapeutic practices, which instead of helping people, put them deeper into this unconscious and self-centered state. In fact, I never thought that a therapist could lead someone to commit suicide until I found out that it was common among Lithuanian psychologists. A proper investigation would put many of them in jail, but I doubt that any government would have the courage to face such a scandal and be known to the rest of the world as a country of psychiatric criminals.

Chapter 24 - Debunking False Paradigms and Embracing Opportunity

We can look at the whole planet and see that fear of confronting problems is just as bad as allowing problems to arise in society, especially when those we trust are the problem - namely the government, the therapists, and the educational system. You do yourself a greater favor by being abnormal in a country where it is normal to be insane. Moreover, governments will never stop the emigration of the healthiest of their citizens if they focus only on the financial situation of their country and not on the state of the culture as well. A country will always be poor as long as it focuses on basic needs, such as money for survival, and not on what drives the satisfaction of those needs, such as honesty and compassion among its people. It is often easier to change our lives and create a new system than to expect change in another system, which is why society is more likely to fail in various ways than to change itself.

Nations make themselves richer by investing in opportunity and a diversity of individual perspectives, and they make themselves poorer by trying to unite everyone under the same values and beliefs, especially if they are religious or political in nature. Opportunity means having the freedom to choose, and that freedom only comes when you are in a rich environment - rich in interactions, different personalities and backgrounds, different values, and so on. If you apply this principle to your personal life, you will find that you grow in the same way - by learning from people with different backgrounds, people with different ideas, and by challenging your beliefs with new beliefs. You grow and change faster when you interact with those who make you question your values, and it is only then that you find a way to be happier that you never considered before. You get there faster through books, travelers, or by becoming a traveler yourself.

On the other hand, if you go to a psychologist who is determined to make you return to the herd from which you came, you are less likely to realize your potential. You should not trust someone just because they have a piece of paper certifying their abilities, academic or otherwise. Systems don't prove anything except the ability to replicate themselves. Instead, you must know what you want and then seek out those who can lead you there.

Everything that happens in life has a dual side from which we transcend by looking at the connections and the lessons we must learn. Only then are we able to create new scenarios where new lessons emerge and from which a new identity is formed based on past understandings, yet aligned with our future goals. In fact, one of the greatest realizations I have gained from traveling to many countries is that we often take the simplest things for granted and they can make a huge difference in how we feel and even how we appreciate life. For example, a beautiful landscape is just part of another day for the locals, but for someone experiencing it for the first time, it is an opportunity to feel blessed to be alive. This is especially true in parts of the world where people are unhappy with their existence because they are too poor, but the land is still beautiful.

It is also interesting to note how easily people close their hearts because of the perceptions of those around them, their own lack of money, and even the travelers they see, for many of those travelers are actually in such places because they find them affordable and pleasant enough to justify trading a year's work for a week's vacation. Likewise, it is interesting to see how different people are who receive a salary from a wealthier country, but choose to live in poor countries because it gives them a better quality of life. In fact, I don't see any reason to live in an expensive nation when many of the most beautiful nations on earth are also the poorest. We seek comfort and a pleasurable life connected to nature, especially near the beach or a tropical forest, or both. Deep down, we find greater happiness in a more connected relationship with nature. This is a form of wealth that cannot be obtained in a rich but cold nation where our lives are nothing more than fulfilling a 9 to 5 routine.

Basically, we want to not have to worry about money and still be able to live where we want and eat what we want, but these characteristics vary with our priorities and what we are willing to sacrifice. Most people have deceived themselves about what they think is important, because the things that are really important don't have a number or a quantity in them. They are all relative to the opportunities we can find. When these opportunities arise, it is foolish not to take advantage of them, and many don't because they are conditioned by old and false paradigms, usually programmed by their parents and society in general. You may often hear people say that rich people are sad, or that money creates loneliness, but that's not true. It is also not true that they despise money, or that they would not play games that give them the idea that they can be rich without effort. But people like to tell themselves stories that help them cope with the routines they can't change, and that's where popular beliefs come from.

never use in his life. Real education should expand the individual's ability to recognize and adapt to new opportunities, and this is possible only through self-education, or more precisely, through books one chooses to read and books in which others share their own life experiences, especially autobiographies.

It is also worth mentioning that if a teacher tries to promote true education in a school, he is immediately ostracized and criticized by his peers, who have been conditioned by the same system to repeat it and not allow anyone to deviate from it. That is why you will not find good teachers in the educational system. Even my own students often criticized me for not using books in the classroom and not writing on the blackboard. They believed that this made me a disorganized and less capable teacher compared to others. But as I explained to them, the books are not adapted to the real world, many of them are outdated, and the methods used in the books are also inferior to what I can provide using a computer connected to the Internet in the classroom, so the only book good enough for me is the one I have created myself and from the many papers I have given them. But then they replied: "But it is easier for us to study with a book!"

I answered them: "You can put together all the lectures I have given you, for each lecture is like a chapter, and you will have a book." But they could not understand this connection between the teaching and a book, because they thought the book was superior to the teaching, as if the book was a Bible that they had to follow religiously. The reason they thought the book was important is because they had been conditioned to see every other teacher in their lives use a book to teach, and never for a moment

Chapter 25 - The Decline of Social Values and the Ris(Complacency

Most people suffer from frustrations that are i with their efforts and inconsistent with their b they should really despise is their own ignorance, whi(itself in their frustrations, with lack of money bei1 obvious. In reality, having more money expands yc possibilities because time and quantity are no longe You can shop more and faster, travel farther, and money than before without much thought or analys need more knowledge to make more money, but you (money to make more mistakes that expand your knov

Knowledge before money is only a creator of p(without opportunities, potential is wasted. Hc institutionalized education offers people is an illusio1 because it reduces the individual's opportunitie: profession and a lot of useless information that the i did any of them question whether that teacher was competent. They assumed that repeating the same model of work made them competent. By comparison, they saw me as incompetent, not the other way around, simply because they thought the many were right and the one who worked differently was wrong. This is a common assumption that people make throughout their lives about everything they observe.

The fact that I write books should be obvious enough as a characteristic that positively differentiates me as a lecturer, because you can't write about what has already been said, but even that they couldn't see. The rest of society does not see this connection between the person and the books in the same way. Many people who ask me how to write books have absolutely nothing new to say. They just want to make themselves feel important by repeating what others have published. We live on a planet of idiots repeating idiocy. No one really analyzes and thinks about all this stupidity, and those who do are considered wrong by everyone else. In such a world, truth is confused with opinion. But truth isn't relative to personal opinion. Only in a world of idiots is truth always relative to quantity, not effectiveness.

People take as true what they see more often, not what works. In fact, people rarely stop to think about the effectiveness of what their politicians say. Instead, they are more likely to follow what they hear, and then blame the politicians for allowing a democratic election, because that's what it is when people blame politicians after voting for them, instead of blaming themselves or those who are too stupid to vote well.

In ancient times, many kings were chosen from among the people on the basis of traits that were considered valuable in their personality. Now people vote for those who make them believe in dreams. In the process, society has lost its sense of purpose. People have become too comfortable with replicating what already exists and trying to keep it as it is, without any changes. In such a society, those who reject it are the most capable of evolving, and yet are often the most insulted, rejected and oppressed.

Chapter 26 - Transcending Dualities and the Stagnation of Religion

One of the most common labels given to children who can't pay attention in class is called ADHD - Attention Deficit Hyperactivity Disorder - which is nothing more than a symptom of someone who is bored because he has to listen to nonsense every day during the most important years of his life when his brain is still developing. ADHD is not a disease, but a normal reaction to an attempt to violate the individual's identity by suppressing his natural development. We don't have an epidemic of mental disorders, we have a huge increase in the distance between technological development (and the opportunities that come with it) and the mental state of the people of this world, who are deliberately kept in a perpetual state of retardation by other retards. This is the real cause of depression and suicide in the world. Because once your brain is made incapable of evolving beyond the lies you have assimilated, you become blind to the changes you want to see.

One of the ways to discover these necessary changes is to read books, but most people are already too numb, apathetic, and demotivated to read anything. When they do read, they usually start with some popular and easily digestible book that obviously repeats more lies, since the only reason a book becomes popular is because it reinforces common beliefs. The worst review I can get as a writer is, "I love this book because it says what I have always believed". The reason this review is terrible is that, first, it says nothing about the quality of the book, and second, the purpose of a book is not to tell you that you are right.

You should read a book not to know if you are right or wrong, as if you were retaking a school exam, but to find new things you were not aware of before, information that will help you make wiser decisions. Anything less is garbage, which is why I don't really read more than half of the books I buy. When I realize that the author is just giving me his personal justifications for what he believes to be true, and then insists on doing it in many different words, as if adding more chapters to the same nonsense makes it more reasonable, I know I'm dealing with a lunatic, and his book is not worth any attention, popular or not, and whether the author is famous or not.

Another very foolish thing I have noticed in many people who claim to read books is that they fall in love with old literature when new literature has completely surpassed almost everything that has ever been written. Many people I've found, especially in religious groups, are so incredibly stupid that they can't believe I write better books than anything they've ever read. They are unable to see that what they have read has already been surpassed by the vast amount of information available today, and that in many cases those authors could not even imagine that it was possible. There is nothing more foolish than to assume that someone who lived a hundred years ago wrote better books than those who live today, and yet that is what the foolish believe.

Technology wasn't as advanced then, books weren't as widely available, there was no such thing as digital information, or the ability to download an entire book in seconds, or to search for words in a book using keywords. It wasn't possible to research information in different books a thousand times faster than before, research methods weren't as advanced or effective as they are today, there weren't as many research papers available as there are today, or as much research being done by as many universities. Yet many people still think those authors wrote better books. You have to be mentally retarded to believe that, which is why I have lost interest in all religions whose members think that way. You really have to be very stupid not to see the difference between the old world and the new world.

The only reason I read many books written thousands of years ago is to compare the two realities and find out how beliefs have changed and how the world became what it is today. The only reason anyone should look at old things is to study history and patterns. This is something that everyone in the field of science knows, but the stupid always think that their idiotic brain is better than the evidence. Then the Freemasons, Rosicrucians, and members of other highly secretive groups ask me how it is possible that I know so much more than they do, as if the things they read are not freely available for anyone to read and understand.

The only secrecy in the world today is not in the knowledge, but in your own lack of ability to understand what you read, or to think that you do when you don't. Self-inflicted misery is the real secret because it's obvious and yet unseen. Many people in this world have learning disabilities. Stupidity is the most widespread disease and also the one that claims the most lives. In every industry, you will see that what causes death was either a personal decision or a collective decision from which people drew rationalizations to avoid punishing themselves. Lawyers are experts at keeping the most dangerous criminals out of jail for the right hourly rate. But the real tragedy is that people violently resist those who try to teach them, as when I show them that they are misinterpreting their own books and they get angry and insult me in response.

The ability to distinguish between the old world and the new world that is changing before our eyes has nothing to do with being a traditionalist or a modernist, and everything to do with having the ability to see how our understanding of life has evolved. Only a fluid mind will see a world in constant change. Only a very ignorant mind will think that life is static, never changing. This is the fundamental difference between seeing the world as a duality of right and wrong and being able to see evolution as a path that transcends dualities and options. On a basic level, the refusal to notice these differences or the inability to compare the two realities can be seen as a lack of discernment or absolute ignorance, but beyond that it is truly a deep state of mental retardation, a deep sleep of the soul.

Some people are literally too slow to see their reality as it is. They live in an imaginary world in their brain, and their religions then look like a composite of all that insanity to make them feel comfortable with what they perceive as external threats to the status quo. I became very bored with the groups I joined because I always had to listen to very basic things that were either common sense or just plain stupid, so I lost respect for all religions, from the most popular to the most occult. It is easy to lose interest in religion when you realize that people act like kindergartners trying to discuss quantum physics based on their beliefs about Peter Pan and Cinderella.

Chapter 27 - The Perverse Cycle of Modern Slavery and the Way Out

You can't talk about spirituality if what you're practicing is a mental ritual in which you try to get pleasure from nonsense without changing your thinking. This is not very different from what you would get if you put several mentally ill people in a room and had a discussion about reality. It is also not very different from what people did thousands of years ago when they tried different cocktails of drugs to try to communicate with God and then wrote books about such experiences, which in many cases became the dogma of the dominant religion. People in such groups think I insulted them by calling them crazy, but I was describing facts - stating observable patterns - that they were not evolved enough to accept because they could not see the same.

They are no different from their ancestors who, thousands of years ago, foolishly repeated rituals based on the ideas of someone tripping on hallucinogenic mushrooms and snake venom as a means of gaining deeper insights into life. The mysticism around sacred drinks that makes up the folklore of most religions, from paganism and Greek mythology to modern Christianity, is nothing more than a ritual around a special drug composed of ingredients no one knows about, much like modern beverage brands like Coca-Cola do when they give people their drink without disclosing the ingredients. In fact, Coca-Cola is nothing more than a ritual-inspired drink that started with the use of real coke leaves, hence the amazing popularity it gained all over the planet. Even the Catholic Pope Leo XIII loved this cocaine drink so much that he helped popularize it in an advertisement of the time. Today, Christians celebrate their mass with wine, which is as much nonsense as anything before, but still a reminder of that past. It is not even surprising that so many writers think they have to be drunk to write well, based on the same ideas. But people always think that the madness was in the past, not in today's world.

If the people around you can't see how distorted their minds and views of reality are, but you can, your only option is to leave them behind. The alternative is to lose every argument with fools who are then determined to make you feel and believe that you are insane by making you doubt everything you say in every way they can. For many years of my life, I thought I was crazy for not knowing that I was more advanced than everyone else I knew. I thought I had something to learn from others, and worse, I thought the people I found in various religions were helping me find the truth. Only much later did I realize that people lie and belittle others to make themselves look right, and will never admit their own insecurities, limitations, and ignorance. People are very insecure, very selfish, and very egotistical. They have no empathy for others because all they want is validation for themselves. Their focus is on a lower nature, although they try to appear holy and spiritual.

This betrayal of my trust forced me to consider myself mentally retarded because for many years I was too naive to see the retardation in others. I could not believe that many people in many different religions could be so selfish, so self-centered, and so evil, and manipulate information to fit those three traits in their personality. It was only when I finally realized this that everything became enlightened to me and I saw how ugly everyone is and I found myself in a horrible world of disgusting monsters obsessed with their own filth. Then I was able to be free because I saw that only I could give myself the answers I needed. This journey, considering how many years we spend being lied to and lost, consumes almost all of our existence. It seems easier to give up, but for me there was no alternative but to create a new world for myself. In fact, the more I know, the less I can live with the filth that others have created for themselves.

Money, of course, becomes very important when you want to get away from this world of madmen, and it's interesting that it's the most viciously attacked topic among them. But you won't get your freedom until you have enough money to buy it. Until then, you will remain a slave to the system. You will need a job, and you will have a salary that barely covers your rent and food, and you will be working for the approval of others to keep that job, so you will not be able to save enough to go anywhere for very long, even if you want to experience a different lifestyle for a while. You will also not have enough time to read books or study new things, let alone learn new languages and develop new skills, because you will be too tired to do any of these things.

This is what slavery really is, it is the exchange of your time and brain for money that does nothing for you except keep you alive so that you can continue to replicate the same system as it is. And because this cycle is so perverse, many of those who awaken go back to sleep when they realize they're in a prison from which they cannot escape. There is an escape, but it requires efforts you have never considered and many sacrifices that can be extremely painful on an emotional and mental level. At the very least, you will have to sacrifice the only free time you have to learn as much as you can, and you will waste much of that time reading the wrong books and listening to the wrong people. By the time you realize where the truth is and what it looks like, you may be in your late forties or fifties, and you will have much less energy than you had before, in your 20s, and yet this is your only chance to experience freedom. You can get there if you can see that the system has weaknesses, gaps created by a constant evolution that requires trustworthy experts. If you position yourself ahead of this evolution, you win.

This is how many people throughout history have become rich. You may agree that selling potatoes, chocolate, sugar, corn, or curry will not make you very rich, but that is how many families became wealthy in the past. Today, people are finding wealth through new opportunities that were unthinkable in the past, such as selling coffee and water bottles. I am sure that new opportunities will continue to emerge and will be more accessible than ever before. The development of the Internet is an example of this, although most people I meet, especially in Europe, are too stupid to understand how someone can make money with a virtual store and, to my amazement, are stupid enough to ridicule such an individual.

Chapter 28 - The Reality of Poor Nations and Miserable Cultures

In today's world, you really have to be very ignorant not to understand how to make money with just a website, yet to my amazement, the vast majority of the population in certain parts of the world don't see how these things are happening in front of their eyes, even when they use such websites themselves. One of the dumbest people I ever met said something that reflects the mentality of people in Europe. She said in reference to one of my companies: "You don't really have a business, you just resell clothes at a higher price and keep a percentage of the profit for yourself".

I looked at her in disbelief because I could not believe that anyone could be so stupid. I asked her in return: "How do you think someone with a business makes money?" She could not answer. But here is the best part: She was an accountant. An accountant who doesn't know how money is made in a business is something I still don't understand. But it's worse than that, like the scientists

I met who were studying the DNA of viruses and didn't know what they were doing and its implications on a larger scale, and this before the coronavirus spread in Europe in 2019. It amazes me that they, being experts, can't see that their research can be used to make bioweapons, and even ridiculed me when I asked about it. People have been made so stupid that they don't understand anything about their own world. When I travel, this becomes so obvious that I have given up asking people the names of streets or even restaurants, because they are never able to tell me about the buildings or streets they pass every day.

For example, recently in Albania, I showed locals a photo of a restaurant and asked where it was, and no one could tell me, not even the owners of a hotel and a hair salon in the same area. They had to use virtual maps on their smartphones to figure out that the restaurant was on the same street where they worked, something I already knew without living there. In fact, that's why I asked them the question. But in the end, these locals were just as useful as I was as a first-time visitor to their country. This should tell you all you need to know about what goes on in people's brains and what I mean when I say they are mentally retarded and useless for anything.

This scenario causes many to have mixed feelings when someone talks about wiping out most of the people on the planet, because they don't see how so many people could be useful as non-thinking, non-hopeful, non-empathetic and non-awakening creatures. At least when people are very stupid and very poor, they might have some compassion for others. But as I have seen in many nations, the opposite happens. They become more selfish, resentful and violent towards those who have what they don't have. The Filipinos in particular are not unhappy because they are poor, but because they lie, manipulate and try to cheat travelers who visit their country. They are extremely rude and extremely corrupt. Not only did I have to pay a huge amount of money to leave their country, but I also had to pay their corrupt employees in government offices to do what their salaries already pay them to do, and this because extortion and corruption is so common in this nation that I have seen every single foreigner in front of me pay at the immigration offices.

The situation is no different at their The Bureau of Immigration at Manila's Ninoy Aquino International Airport, where Filipino travelers are constantly being turned away from boarding a flight for not paying the person who is abusing his position and asking very personal questions. They are so used to it that when I did not give the immigration officer any money for literally printing a paper to leave a country where I was not even born but merely a visitor, he asked: "Where is my money?" Worse than being poor is being a liar and a cheat. What a wretched nation this is, even though they claim to be majority Christian.

Comparable to the Filipinos are the Lithuanians and the Poles, whose misery has only become less obvious since they joined the European Union. On their own, they would remain as miserable as they have always been, because a terrible culture and a people without positive values make for a miserable nation. And nothing is more obvious than their lack of gratitude to those who helped them to develop out of misery, because that is exactly how a miserable people appreciates the help received, by claiming that they did everything on their own and are superior to everyone else. This attitude only reinforces the need of some to exterminate them instead of helping them, and makes it very difficult to think about evolution from the bottom up, or to feel compassion for such people when their nation is destroyed by a foreign invasion.

The human race is a problem when it refuses to evolve or is denied such evolution, which is why the system is antagonistic to itself. The more people are immersed in the system and the more they trust it, the more useless they become as human beings and the more they suffer as victims of the system they protect. This is why nationalism is the way a stupid people protect collective beliefs that should be changed. Nationalism is the crystallization of a people under a territory and symbolized by a flag. It makes no sense in a constantly evolving scenario. But worse is racism, the idea that your nation is not made up of a multitude of peoples from different parts of the world, but a single crop of people cultivated in the potato fields of this land by some mysterious force called God.

Those who escape the system are actually the most necessary elements for it. But you don't have to believe me. The many job offers I have received without asking prove my point. People want someone like me to run their businesses, to teach them and their teachers pedagogy, to speak in public and help them develop a business strategy. They don't want to work with or learn from those who have nothing to say or offer except a repetition of what people instinctively know doesn't work well. And yet the irony is that I am as needed as I am hated. People want to know as much as possible about what I know and are equally energetic in rejecting everything I say. They are as proud to admire me for what I have accomplished as they are creative in insulting me for not being able to do the same.

Chapter 29 - The Hard Truth About Parental Responsibility and Success

The interesting thing about evolving as a human being is that you soon realize that it is not just a decision that affects your intelligence and social life, but that it is really a completely organic change. For example, I changed my diet several times to reduce my depression levels and to keep me focused and less sick for longer periods of time. I also started exercising more because I saw the connection between how my brain worked and my ability to think effectively.

Money became essential in my life to travel more and longer distances, which then helps me stay more focused while observing new ways of living and thinking. In essence, everything in my life became part of who I am, which is why I think people who tell me to relax and work less are stupid. If I thought like them, I would have their life, not mine. They can't have my life because they refuse to think like me. They want my life with their way of thinking, and that's what stupidity is - it's wanting to progress without changing yourself.

Morality is in line with this progress, because you are more likely to produce better products and sell more easily if you are trustworthy and understand the needs of your customers, which is why I maintain a direct relationship with my readers with authenticity, respecting their interests and questions.

Along the way, I have also had to learn to accept that some things are not compatible with this new lifestyle, including a stable social life. I am more likely to meet people I will never see again than to have long-term friends at this point, and I have learned to accept that as a positive rather than a negative. Most people are not very unique anyway, so the more people you meet, the more you realize that they are incapable of changing, repeating the same mindset, beliefs, and conversations for many decades. Intelligent, unique and kind people are rare. With this in mind, the abundance that you then reflect upon others, and which is abnormal to them, becomes nothing more than normal to you.

For example, people always ask me how I make friends so fast, but considering that they all disappear, especially after I travel, and never answer my messages again, I don't see it as making many friends, but simply meeting many people along the way. People also ask me why I care so much about money, because they clearly don't see the connection between productivity, money and expenses, and you should actually want to maximize your profits to work less for the results, not more, while also reducing your expenses so you don't have to work more. They don't understand this because they trade their life for time. They don't value time or freedom enough to respect someone who does. That's why they don't value money while claiming to want more of it. You can't get what you don't respect. This is as true of people as it is of money, because people invented money to facilitate transactions in a highly dysfunctional, immoral, and selfish world where bartering was too difficult and time-consuming, and theft and corruption were everywhere, just as they are today. It's precisely because people lack moral qualities that money is so important. But most people just don't seem to understand these things, they don't understand how their own lives work.

Basically, if money were bad, homeless people would be the happiest people in the world. Besides, isn't it amazing to see that we have evolved over so many thousands of years to come to a world where most people have no idea how it works, how money is made, or how potatoes are planted and grown, nothing, no knowledge of anything useful, not even of their own history as a people. But the observations we make in the reality we have also define our choices, so when people see less, they also have no understanding of these things, even if you try to explain it to them.

One of the stupidest and most common consequences of this mass ignorance is the obsession with genetic associations. People really think that the man who provided the sperm and the woman who provided the egg during a moment of sex are individuals to be worshipped and emotionally attached to for the rest of their lives. They don't see that this correlation is relative to what those two individuals did to promote the survival and success of their sons and daughters in life, and that in many cases what they did was the exact opposite. It sounds offensive to say these things to many people, but the truth is that most parents are nothing more than losers who repeat the same mentality of ignorance to the next generations. They deserve nothing in return. The only parents who deserve anything from their sons and daughters are those who sacrifice their existence to provide a better education for the next generation and encourage their sons and daughters to work harder and persevere regardless of their results. I have seen this in Chinese and Indian families, but I haven't seen it in other parts of the world.

Often the excuse is that the family doesn't have enough money to give their children a proper education, in which case I think they shouldn't have children. This is not a negative way of looking at life, but a practical and positive way. In fact, if we have to explain the concept of being positive, I would say that it is not based on the positive aspect of it, but on the ability to differentiate states of mind and how they lead to very different results and behaviors, because you cannot justify negative facts when they are obviously bad. It's actually interesting that in Filipino culture, children are called selfish and immoral if they don't want to help their family by giving them part of their salary, when the opposite is true: if you were conceived in poverty, you don't owe anything to people who couldn't control themselves and were selfish and immoral enough to bring you to life during an act of pleasure for their bodies. How can a child owe its life to two people for no other reason than they had sex? It makes no sense, except on a planet of very mentally ill people.

Chapter 30 - Making Informed Decisions in a World of Psychopaths

Sometimes a behavior that can be perceived as negative can lead to a positive outcome, while a behavior that can be perceived as positive can lead to a negative behavior. For example, if a British woman in front of me on the bus is frantically clutching her purse as if I am going to rob her, she sees this as a positive behavior that I see as offensive and extremely stupid. She doesn't know that she is acting like a mental retard because to a mental retard the color of a person's skin determines what you can expect from them. A negative behavior with positive influences would be to insult this woman and teach her a lesson about discrimination by discriminating against her because of her lack of intelligence. But many people cannot see the difference between the two situations, and that is why many injustices are committed in the name of law and religion. We see this when the United States and NATO invade countries using lies as excuses and no one complains, but then people react when Russia does the same to other nations, even when it has a valid excuse for doing so.

This hypocrisy accompanied by a lack of discernment of reality is also manifested in the way people look at themselves, as they often think that it is because the rich have too much that they have too little. But we can analyze this on a smaller scale, like when someone asks me for a job and then demands a very high salary. Why should I pay more for things that haven't even been done? What I've noticed with many people is that they don't like to work, they just believe that those who have more should share more, but where did my money come from? Wasn't it from my own work? You see, there is an element of selfishness behind what appears to be a socialistic view of life. People believe they are entitled to things without doing anything to earn them.

As more and more people struggle with unemployment and then try to make a living from tourism, I began to notice the same pattern again. That is, I'm tricked into booking an apartment that looks like it has everything I paid for, and when I arrive I see something else: rusty furniture, a house that's not well cleaned, nothing I can use to cook food, or too old to be used, and so on. Then these people get very angry when I decide to leave the next day and demand a refund. They never, in any case that I have ever found, want to return the money. They truly believe that this money is theirs and not the result of a transaction that never happened because they were too lazy to clean the house and did the minimum possible to keep a customer. In many cases, they thought it was unfair that I decided to leave. What hope do these people have?

Their purpose in life is to scam as many people as possible because that is how they see the idea of making a living. It is even worse when popular rental websites encourage this behavior because they have the exact same mindset and then delete any negative reviews that warn customers of these situations. In this way, such companies are able to scam as many people as possible, even if the clients are robbed and raped in the apartments they rent, which has often been the case.

People then say that the problem of the world is the lack of jobs, because they only see the surface. They don't see that most people are unfit to be part of society and that their existence is a source of problems. I've been poor in many moments of my life, and I've never used that condition to justify lying and cheating, so I don't think it can be used as an excuse. In fact, it's because of these people that stricter laws are justified. In a world of sane people, there would be no need for laws, because common sense and honesty would be the most important and only known laws. It is a mentally ill society that sees immorality as a shortcut to more profit. The many psychopaths I have met in different parts of the world and from different professions show me this when they say: "What do you care about other people? What they do with what you tell them is their problem!"

We can then conclude that it is not what we have that makes the difference, but how we live our lives. I am referring, of course, to the choices we make along the way and the direction they take us. And of course, knowing the facts about the environment in which our choices are made can lead us to a better outcome. For example, it would be foolish to try to have an honest career in countries where the majority of people are psychopathic. In such countries, you are more likely to become rich and famous through violence or its counterpart, working with the military or private security companies.

It may sound ridiculous to say that being part of the military can make you rich, until you look at countries like Portugal and realize that their military is so corrupt that they can turn any illegal process into a legal one and keep important people involved in arms trafficking out of jail. I have never heard of a single case in that country where the military has arrested anyone for criminal activity within the army. On the contrary, in Portugal, if you tell others that you work for the military, people respect you, because in a country where the majority is psychopathic, those who abuse power tend to be the most respected.

For the same reason, their politicians are often caught in corruption and money laundering schemes, but rarely if ever go to jail. Worse, the population is stupid enough to re-elect those who have served time to the exact same political office they held before. In many other cases, they continue to have political influence despite legal problems and jail time. An uneducated people really shows up in stupid decisions. But if you want to take care of bureaucratic issues in this country, they treat you as if you are trying to gain the trust of honest people. This is also how psychopaths hide their imbecility, because many of the workers in government offices have no idea what they are doing or what the law says, and if you hire a lawyer in this country, he will lie about your rights in order to extort as much money from you as he can, because he has even less regard for the law than anyone else. It is also not uncommon for a Portuguese lawyer to try to get more profit from the people you are fighting against so that you lose the case with them. You can save more money by hiring a detective to follow your lawyer around, find incriminating evidence against him, and make sure he does his job properly.

Chapter 31 - The Value of Discretion and Strategic Investment

How you interpret and observe the world determines the direction your life will take, so you can't expect others to agree with you as you evolve. For example, most people interpret my existence in a very different way than it actually is. Many people assume that I write books to travel, and not that I chose to write books to stop working as a teacher or a business manager or any other job that would force me to stay in the same place with the same people every day. That's a sickness for me and unbearable, especially when I didn't choose those people and have to pretend to tolerate them every day.

People also think that my purpose is to go everywhere on the planet and not that I move when I'm unhappy and can't solve visa problems. It is actually very difficult to get a visa to stay in almost any country on the planet, especially if you are financially independent, because countries want your money, not you, and unless that money is invested in large quantities - in completely irrelevant and useless things - they won't give you a permit to stay. In the end, it will be much cheaper to travel than to stay somewhere as a resident. For the cost of the golden visa in Greece, for example, you could take a private jet and fly around the planet, and you still would not have spent half the money.

Another thing that most people don't seem to realize because they keep thinking like their grandparents is that in today's world it is not a good investment to buy a house unless you are not going to live in it but rent it out to someone else. You probably won't pay it off in a lifetime, and the upkeep just doesn't make up for having it. You are better off investing that money in various rental properties throughout your life. What is worth doing in today's world is to invest in knowledge because it is now much more accessible and very inexpensive, and to invest in a business that can be automated so that you can be free of the responsibilities within a few years and then earn passive income from it. And if you can do that multiple times, you can live a very good life.

However, as I observe, the vast majority of the population is completely unaware of these things. One of the things that people cannot see about me, for example, is that writing books is not just a way of life or a business, it is a formula, because these books will sell forever, even though they are only written once. That's eternal income from a job done in a few days. But of course there are other examples that can be compared to this, in the field of digital art, video, photography and music, and many individuals are actually seeing these opportunities, while the rest of the people seem to be asleep to everything that is happening, namely the many developments in artificial intelligence that can replicate art at the highest level.

When we observe that people are slow to change, and in many cases not changing at all, we often fail to see the full extent of this reality, because what it means is that the masses are still following the same thought patterns of their ancestors who lived without the Internet, without electricity, and without many of the opportunities that we have today. I still see people in cafes reading paper books at the speed of a snail, which is the dumbest thing I can imagine doing today. Maybe they think they are very smart by reading a book in public, but the real smart thing is to put on headphones and listen to books while relaxing your eyes by looking at an ocean or a lake and relaxing your mind. This is how I get through dozens of books a day without anyone noticing what I am doing. You will get much further in life if you stop caring what others think and reject the idea that you have to prove anything to them.

For example, posting a photo of yourself with a Lamborghini or a boat on social media may get you praise from your friends and the kind of validation you're looking for from them, but it's much more valuable to your future to keep your mouth shut, not show anything about what you're doing, let people think you're poor and stupid and maybe even selling drugs, as many assume about me, and then judge them according to the judgments they make about you while you're making important decisions that they can't even see or understand, which is what I do all the time. Then take the money that could be spent on that Lamborghini and use it to invest in starting businesses, a real estate project, and hiring people to work for you. At an average cost of one to two thousand dollars a month, you can employ almost anyone from around the world for many years if you can afford a Lamborghini. And if you choose your employees wisely and give them a functional project, they will make you richer, which will justify their salary and allow you to hire even more people. If you live in a poor country, poverty is your advantage because you can hire more people for less money and get your results faster than anyone else in the world.

Chapter 32 - Focus on Quality and the People Who Appreciate It

For someone who has achieved wealth in his life, the very silly thing to do is to post photos of your cars on social media and seek validation from others, because at that point, everyone will come asking you for money or complaining if you don't give it to them. Along the way, you may think you need other people's approval, but it is worthless, that is the wrong goal. If you can't keep your mouth shut about your goals or wealth, you are probably not qualified to be wealthy. You know you are qualified to be very rich when you don't seek other people's company, respect or approval, and you don't even need to know what they think. When you don't care what other people think, you gain more space in your mind to formulate your own thoughts, many of which will be completely new and more focused on your future than on your present.

In my case, for example, I never really thought about owning a boat until I started traveling a lot more and realized that a yacht would save me money and headaches related to dealing with scammers who rent horrible apartments. The most popular platforms related to hosting travelers provide very poor service in an industry used by millions. But the real problem is that few people travel all year, not just a few weeks out of the year, so people like me are better off using boats than second-rate apartments advertised as luxury homes. In this case, I'm talking about a yacht as a means to save money and be more practical in life, with more comfort, rather than as a means to gain social validation, and that's the part that many, especially the poor, can't understand. The poor always focus on external aspects because they have no concept of essence, planning or vision.

I could say the same thing about those who ask me how to make money with books and music, as if it doesn't matter how smart and talented they are, because they will never reach my level of success, and they will never reach it for a very simple reason that they cannot understand: They are trying to get it from a selfish and poor mindset. They see money as their goal, not the quality of their work and the people who will pay for it. This is why they fail and will always fail, and why they deserve to fail. Whenever I want to make more money, I don't focus on the money, I focus on my work. I try to find ways to improve the quality of what I do, and I have re-released some of my best-selling books after improving them. I have also re-released my music after working on the equalization of the sounds in each of them.

Despite all this, much of my work doesn't produce the results I expect, but I am consistent with this principle, and that is why I have been a successful full-time artist and author for over ten years, and have traveled to dozens of countries based on this mindset and consistency. Other people, the vast majority, can't see things this way. They're too obsessed with the money part, which is why I can't even talk to them. The more I know about how life works, the fewer friends I have, because most people are just too stupid, too insulting, too arrogant, and too jealous for people like me to associate with or even teach them anything they need to learn. The majority can only be with others like them because they are unable to accept anyone who thinks better than they do. They are too self-centered to tolerate such a person.

This is why many of my past relationships failed and why many people cannot find a real relationship. If most people can't live without going to the beach for a weekend, if they can't stop getting drunk all the time, if they can't say the word "no" to a party, then they can't be a part of my life, and likewise, when the time comes for me to spend a whole year on an island enjoying the sun, I'll have to do that part alone.

It is sad to say, and often unbearable for many to read, but most people are incapable of evolving, although their misery is a consequence of their stupidity and bad choices, and they tend to be too stupid because they are greedy and lazy. So should I feel sorry for them? I feel sorry for those who read a lot and work hard and don't get what they want, but I have never met a single person who reads a lot and works a lot and doesn't get what he wants. In fact, I have never met a person who works hard, reads a lot of mental health books, and suffers from mental illness. It doesn't happen! Once you become determined to solve your problems, you find the answers, you find the right people to help you, and then you solve everything. The law of manifestation or attraction is real, you attract what you focus on, but only if you are willing to work for it and are open to receiving it.

We tend to think that we are in control of our destiny and that we can make our own choices, but what we do control are our thoughts, decisions and actions, and they are constantly aligned with the perceived reality, which is the same as the person the thoughts create. Therefore, we can never change our reality until we first change our thoughts. These thoughts are not changed by decisions, but by perceptions, and perceptions are the seeds we plant in our minds as we accumulate a vast amount of perspectives and information.

Chapter 33 - Finding True Faith Beyond Organized Belief

The potential to change our destiny by changing our thoughts applies to wealth as well as happiness and mental health. It is in the process of changing from within that any manifestation or miracle truly occurs. I know this because I have seen it in my own life. I have been homeless, I have lost all my savings several times, and God has made money come into my life, made opportunities and ideas come into my life, and made many other incredible and completely unexpected things happen to help me change my destiny. The people in my life did nothing to help me, even when they had the chance, so I can only feel sick thinking about them. I have removed everyone I met from my life because I despise people who cannot help and refuse to help for no other reason than their selfishness, and that includes not offering the living room or couch to a friend who has no place to go. I really despise that!

Now I live in large apartments, often with several rooms available, and I sleep in only one and invite no one to enjoy it with me.

That's my own revenge! In fact, it is more correct to say that this is God's revenge through me, because without faith nothing would be possible. And contrary to what the many delusional fools of Christianity think, this faith has nothing to do with religion - it is a direct relationship between me and God. Especially in my case, if I had to rely on religion for help, I would be very unhappy, because none of the many religions I have been to have ever helped me with anything.

If you want to build a faith around a religion, then wrap it around the faith that is revealed in my books, which, as you can see, has nothing to do with any organized religion in the world. There is no other way, religion or profession, that will help you get maximum results because what I'm revealing already contains the most realistic approach to miracles. Faith is the only thing you need in life, although many people claim they can't enjoy life without a plasma screen or a big car, and once they have these things, they just want more of the same or bigger sizes. This constant need, like a parasite feeding on anxiety and depression, makes them miserable, and yet they somehow feel comfortable in their life cycle because they don't understand any other way of experiencing life.

For example, many Europeans spend a whole year saving money to go to Asia for fifteen days, while Asians spend a whole year saving money to go to Europe for fifteen days. Meanwhile, most people from the countryside feel bored with their lives and want to travel to the big cities to enjoy their time there, while those in such cities feel so anxious and stressed by the constant movement that they want to relax in the countryside. There must be something terribly wrong with the way we interpret life, because everyone seems confused about what they want and need, and how to satisfy such needs and wants. The answer will not come without proper introspection into who we are, and this leads us to another common misconception, which is that we must appreciate and love life before we can appreciate and love ourselves, and not the other way around.

The contradictory behaviors trap too many people in a paradox that makes no sense, and their emotions tell them so. But loving yourself is about doing and being what makes you respect yourself, and that's where many people fail, precisely because they expect others to give them such respect. For example, if a person says, "I'm not beautiful enough," the answer is, "Make yourself beautiful!"; if she says, "I don't have enough money," the answer is, "Find cheaper quality clothes that will make you feel better!"; if someone says, "I'm not confident enough," the answer is, "Listen to music that makes you feel good, and relax in a park, listen to the birds sing, and try to meet new people!" Finally, if a person says, "I don't have enough friends to go out with," the answer is, "Join clubs, associations, sports activities, or start your own group until you have enough friends!"

Most people are so wrapped up in their thinking patterns and what others see in them that they can't find these opportunities and then create more barriers for themselves. But the ability to develop more self-esteem is the first and most important step in healing the mind. This is why a walk in the park can work wonders for the most depressed person and help open their mind to new possibilities. Many of the best ideas I have ever had came in moments of despair, when I simply stopped and relaxed my mind. As a person feels more confident and self-reliable with these activities, it is then possible to develop a better inner understanding, and it is from this center that we find what we need to do with our lives.

Chapter 34 - Understanding the Levels of Social Integration

If we were to draw a scale of what should be normal, we would get the following:

Level 0 - Being nothing.

Level 1 - The need to exist.

Level 2 - The need to be seen by society.

Level 3 - The need to contribute to society.

Level 4 - The need to be a part of society.

Level 5 - The need to be of value to society.

Level 6 - The need to be seen as an influential element of society.

What is wrong with the world today is that people want to be at the sixth level, but spend most of their time thinking at the first level. They do this by wasting time taking too many pictures of themselves, spending too much time on social media, and trying to make their appearance noticeable to others. As a result, they get further and further away from what they want in life. Then comes the false sense of entitlement, the belief that one has a right to a job and a good salary and a family - which would place a person in Levels Four and Five - except that such an individual lacks the social skills to interact with the rest of society on a healthy level.

When these individuals finally realize they have a problem, they can't even see what the problem is because they are too focused on Level Zero - being nothing. They then want their therapist to tell them who they are, and that's what they spend the next few months talking about, but while a good therapist would try to make the patient understand their personality, in this state the patient is mostly looking for attention. And that's why both therapist and patient tend to go nowhere. Should the therapist care about this situation? No, because he gets paid for the attention he gives. Should the patient care about his situation? No, because he is paying for the attention himself. In fact, most people say the following about their psychologists: "It's great to have someone you can talk to openly."

This explains the failure of therapy, which could be corrected if every therapist had a supervisor to whom they had to explain their failures. But they don't, because therapy is fundamentally an arbitrary and subjective process, as many studies have shown. Therapists draw conclusions that are often based more on personal opinion than fact. But if both therapist and patient are happy with the outcome, and despite the lack of results, can we really say that there is something wrong with it?

An angry reaction is normal and to be expected when we realize that we have been deceived for many years, and it is better to be angry than to be depressed without answers. Anger always follows a state of depression, but it is natural, it represents the awareness of a need for self-validation over social validation. In fact, this self-validation often contradicts the values needed for social validation, which is why it attracts an inner conflict-an anger directed at the world that reflects anger at oneself. It is a manifestation of a lack of self-love, which manifests as frustration.

The problem only persists when this need is sought outwardly, as when people strive to be accepted by others because it is unlikely to ever happen. People won't apologize, change, or make excuses for what they have done to you, and are more likely to disappear when confronted with their past actions and words. If we need to find a way outside ourselves to balance the inside, then the activities that better bridge the gap are those that allow some form of direct contact with our inner alchemy, such as exercise, a deeper relationship with nature, and meditation, and especially a combination of all three: like hiking up a mountain in the early morning and meditating at the top. A simple bike ride, for example, can also help alleviate depression. In essence, we want to keep ourselves active with the right elements, because it is the combination of action and chemistry that improves our overall mental health.

When I say "the right elements," I am referring not only to those that are external to you, but also to those that are internal, such as helping yourself more quickly to fresh fruits, vegetables, and nuts. These are foods that are rich in positive energy. Even if you want to address your thoughts directly, we already know that they are better organized when they are directed toward a goal, which is why you get more clarity from an activity than from lying in bed depressed and thinking about life. No matter how complex your life may seem, you will heal faster if you get into the habit of having more action in your life - action that is aligned with space, nature, and time. This means that the more you do in natural environments, the faster you heal and the clearer your mind becomes. You will then be able to see the solutions that you could not see before.

Chapter 35 - Healing Through Connection and Externalization

A question that often comes up is how do we get someone who is mentally ill to want to move and do things? Isn't that a contradiction of their condition? Each person needs a unique solution, but the individual doesn't really heal by mirroring himself and his condition. This healing occurs only when the person understands the connection between himself and the outside world. It is a process of assimilating reality through exteriorization of the mind or personal attention.

One of the common problems with people who are depressed is that they very easily adapt to negative cycles, habits and routines, and even become obsessed with these cycles as a way of escaping any introspection. For example, someone who is depressed because she is unemployed will become obsessed with getting a job and will not have the clarity of mind to try to improve her curriculum. She will also try to get a job out of fear rather than out of a genuine interest in the interview and what she should be doing. And with such behaviors, this person ends up further separating herself from the opportunities she seeks.

The more dependent people are on external validation, the more psychological and emotional challenges they will acquire. Solidarity and supportive friendships would prevent such a situation, but most people don't help their friends when they are in need, and that is the real problem here. Society is more focused on selfish needs and self-gratification than on compassion.

Mental health problems are as much a result of a dysfunctional and unhealthy world as they are a problem to be solved by it. When the world fails the individual, he has few, if any, other alternatives to escape negative cycles, and the more he looks outside himself, the more likely he is to encounter frustrations, challenges, barriers, and other obstacles to his own self-development.

When what is perceived as normal becomes part of a culture and is even praised by the people who protect it, an individual is condemned to a darkness of ignorance from which he can only escape by seeking new knowledge, new insights, and new ways of experiencing reality with a fresh perspective. This is as true for mental health as it is for achieving a richer and more prosperous lifestyle. You are more likely to achieve your goals if you separate yourself from the beliefs of others and form your own, including the beliefs you were raised to trust about yourself.

This may seem abnormal to everyone you meet, for if what is normal is abnormal, then what is truly normal will be seen as abnormal by those who are abnormal themselves. This state that others perceive as abnormal will keep you sane, and in time it will help you to align your future with your true self in the center of your heart. This is how you will find a life worth living, a life that truly inspires you to wake up in the morning, rejoice with the sound of the birds, and become a better version of yourself.

Glossary of Terms

Covert Antisocial Behavior: Deceptive and manipulative actions taken by individuals with an abnormal mindset, such as lying, cheating, and exploiting others in order to survive and gain an advantage.

Dual Worldview: A simplistic, binary perspective that divides the world into "us versus them," "predator versus prey," or "aggressor versus victim," rather than recognizing the complexity and interconnectedness of human relationships and society.

Emotional Brainwashing: The process of manipulating someone's emotions, often by using fear, shame, and insecurity to control their thoughts and behaviors.

Evolutionary Trajectory: The idea that human beings are on a continuous path of personal and societal development, with some individuals and cultures being more "evolved" than others in terms of their level of self-awareness, empathy, and ability to cooperate.

Gaslighting: A form of psychological manipulation in which the perpetrator causes the victim to question his or her own reality, memory, or perceptions, often by denying or contradicting the victim's experiences.

Illusions: False beliefs or perceptions that individuals hold about themselves, others, and the world around them that can lead to irrational and self-destructive behavior.

Introversion: A psychological state in which an individual has internalized his or her own view of the world and struggles to change it when interacting with reality, often resulting in narcissism and a lack of empathy.

Narcissism: An excessive preoccupation with one's own self-importance, often accompanied by a fragile sense of self-worth and a need to constantly validate and protect one's ego.

Organic Change: The idea that personal growth and transformation are not merely intellectual exercises, but involve a holistic, interconnected process that affects all aspects of an individual's life, including physical, emotional, and social well-being.

Predatory Mindset: A mindset that focuses on dominating and exploiting others, often at the expense of their well-being, in order to ensure one's own survival and success.

Psychopathy: A personality disorder characterized by a lack of empathy, a disregard for the rights and feelings of others, and a tendency to engage in manipulative and antisocial behavior.

Reciprocity: The mutual exchange of thoughts, feelings, and actions between individuals that is essential to the development of healthy relationships and social connections.

Reptilian Brain: A metaphorical term used to describe the more primitive, instinctual aspects of the human mind that can lead to aggressive, selfish, and survival-oriented behavior.

Self-reflection: The ability to critically examine one's thoughts, beliefs, and behaviors and recognize how they may be influenced by unconscious biases, societal conditioning, and past experiences.

Social Mask: The persona an individual adopts to conform to societal norms and expectations, often at the expense of their true self and authentic expression.

Survival Mechanisms: The psychological and behavioral strategies individuals use to ensure their own safety and well-being, often at the expense of others.

Book Review Request

Dear reader,

Thank you for purchasing this book! I would love to know your opinion. Writing a book review helps in understanding the readers and also impacts other readers' purchasing decisions. Your opinion matters. Please write a book review!

Your kindness is greatly appreciated!

About the Author

Dan Desmarques is a renowned author with a remarkable track record in the literary world. With an impressive portfolio of 28 Amazon bestsellers, including eight #1 bestsellers, Dan is a respected figure in the industry. Drawing on his background as a college professor of academic and creative writing, as well as his experience as a seasoned business consultant, Dan brings a unique blend of expertise to his work. His profound insights and transformational content appeal to a wide audience, covering topics as diverse as personal growth, success, spirituality, and the deeper meaning of life. Through his writing, Dan empowers readers to break free from limitations, unlock their inner potential, and embark on a journey of self-discovery and transformation. In a competitive self-help market, Dan's exceptional talent and inspiring stories make him a standout author, motivating readers to engage with his books and embark on a path of personal growth and enlightenment.

Also Written by the Author

1. 66 Days to Change Your Life: 12 Steps to Effortlessly Remove Mental Blocks, Reprogram Your Brain and Become a Money Magnet

2. A New Way of Being: How to Rewire Your Brain and Take Control of Your Life

3. Abnormal: How to Train Yourself to Think Differently and Permanently Overcome Evil Thoughts

4. Alignment: The Process of Transmutation Within the Mechanics of Life

5. Audacity: How to Make Fast and Efficient Decisions in Any Situation

6. Beyond Belief: Discovering Sacred Moments in Everyday Life

7. Beyond Illusions: Discovering Your True Nature

8. Beyond Self-Doubt: Unleashing Boundless Confidence for Extraordinary Living

9. Breaking Free from Samsara: Achieving Spiritual Liberation and Inner Peace

10. Breakthrough: Embracing Your True Potential in a Changing World

11. Christ Cult Codex: The Untold Secrets of the Abrahamic Religions and the Cult of Jesus

12. Codex Illuminatus: Quotes & Sayings of Dan Desmarques

13. Collective Consciousness: How to Transcend Mass Consciousness and Become One With the Universe

14. Creativity: Everything You Always Wanted to Know About How to Use Your Imagination to Create Original Art That People Admire

15. Deception: When Everything You Know about God is Wrong

16. Demigod: What Happens When You Transcend The Human Nature?

17. Discernment: How Do Your Emotions Affect Moral Decision-Making?

18. Design Your Dream Life: A Guide to Living Purposefully

19. Eclipsing Mediocrity: How to Unveil Hidden Realities and Master Life's Challenges

20. Energy Vampires: How to Identify and Protect Yourself

21. Fearless: Powerful Ways to Get Abundance Flowing into Your Life

22. Feel, Think and Grow Rich: 4 Elements to Attract Success in Life

23. Find More with Less: Uncluttering Your Mind, Body, and Soul

24. Find Your Flow: How to Get Wisdom and Knowledge from God

25. Hacking the Universe: The Revolutionary Way to Achieve Your Dreams and Unleash Your True Power

26. Holistic Psychology: 77 Secrets about the Mind That They Don't Want You to Know

27. How to Change the World: The Path of Global Ascension Through Consciousness

28. How to Get Lucky: How to Change Your Mind and Get Anything in Life

29. How to Improve Your Self-Esteem: 34 Essential Life Lessons Everyone Should Learn to Find Genuine Happiness

30. How to Study and Understand Anything: Discovering The Secrets of the Greatest Geniuses in History

31. How to Spot and Stop Manipulators: Protecting Yourself and Reclaiming Your Life

32. Intuition: 5 Keys to Awaken Your Third Eye and Expand Spiritual Perception

33. Karma Mastery: Transforming Life's Lessons into Conscious Creations

34. Legacy: How to Build a Life Worth Remembering

35. Master Your Emotions: The Art of Intentional Living

36. Mastering Alchemy: The Key to Success and Spiritual Growth

37. Metanoia Mechanics: The Secret Science of Profound Mental Shifts

38. Metamorphosis: 16 Catalysts for Unconventional Growth and Transformation

39. Mindshift: Aligning Your Thoughts for a Better Life

40. Mind Over Madness: Strategies for Thriving Amidst Chaos

41. Money Matters: A Holistic Approach to Building Financial Freedom and Well-Being

42. Quantum Leap: Unleashing Your Infinite Potential

43. Religious Leadership: The 8 Rules Behind Successful Congregations

44. Reset: How to Observe Life Through the Hidden Dimensions of Reality and Change Your Destiny

45. Resilience: The Art of Confronting Reality Against the Odds

46. Raise Your Frequency: Aligning with Higher Consciousness

47. Revelation: The War Between Wisdom and Human Perception

48. Spiritual Anarchist: Breaking the Chains of Consensual Delusion

49. Spiritual DNA: Bridging Science and Spirituality to Live Your Best Life

50. Spiritual Warfare: What You Need to Know About Overcoming Adversity

51. Starseed: Secret Teachings about Heaven and the Future of Humanity

52. Stupid People: Identifying, Analyzing and Overcoming Their Toxic Influence

53. Technocracy: The New World Order of the Illuminati

and The Battle Between Good and Evil

54. The 10 Laws of Transmutation: The Multidimensional Power of Your Subconscious Mind

55. The 14 Karmic Laws of Love: How to Develop a Healthy and Conscious Relationship With Your Soulmate

56. The 33 Laws of Persistence: How to Overcome Obstacles and Upgrade Your Mindset for Success

57. The 36 Laws of Happiness: How to Solve Urgent Problems and Create a Better Future

58. The Alchemy of Truth: Embracing Change and Transcending Time

59. The Altruistic Edge: Succeeding by Putting Others First

60. The Antagonists: What Makes a Successful Person Different?

61. The Antichrist: The Grand Plan of Total Global Enslavement

62. The Art of Letting Go: Embracing Uncertainty and Living a Fulfilling Life

63. The Awakening: How to Turn Darkness Into Light and Ascend to Higher Dimensions of Existence

64. The Egyptian Mysteries: Essential Hermetic Teachings for a Complete Spiritual Reformation

65. The Dark Side of Progress: Navigating the Pitfalls of Technology and Society

66. The Evil Within: The Spiritual Battle in Your Mind Deception: When Everything You Know about God is Wrong

67. The Game of Life and How to Play It: How to Get Anything You Want in Life

68. The Hidden Language of God: How to Find a Balance Between Freedom and Responsibility

69. The Mosaic of Destiny: Deciphering the Patterns of Your Life

70. The Most Powerful Quotes: 400 Motivational Quotes and Sayings

71. The Multidimensional Nature of Reality: Transcending the Limits of the Human Mind

72. The Secret Beliefs of The Illuminati: The Complete Truth About Manifesting Money Using The Law of Attraction That is Being Hidden From You

73. The Secret Empire: The Hidden Truth Behind the Power Elite and the Knights of the New World Order

74. The Secret Science of the Soul: How to Transcend Common Sense and Get What You Really Want From Life

75. The Spiritual Laws of Money: The 31 Best-kept Secrets to Life-long Abundance

76. The Spiritual Mechanics of Love: Secrets They Don't Want You to Know about Understanding and Processing Emotions

77. The Universal Code: Understanding the Divine Blueprint

78. The Unknown: Exploring Infinite Possibilities in a Conformist World

79. The Narcissist's Secret: Why They Hate You (and What to Do About It)

80. Thrive: Spark Creativity, Overcome Obstacles and Unleash Your Potential

81. Transcend: Embracing Change and Overcoming Life's Challenges

82. Uncharted Paths: Pursuing True Fulfillment Beyond Society's Expectations

83. Uncompromised: The Surprising Power of Integrity in a Corrupt World

84. Unacknowledged: How Negative Emotions Affect Your Mental Health?

85. Unapologetic: Taking Control of Your Mind for a

Happier and Healthier Life

86. Unbreakable: Turning Hardship into Opportunity

87. Uncommon: Transcending the Lies of the Mental Health Industry

88. Unlocked: How to Get Answers from Your Subconscious Mind and Control Your Life

89. Why do good people suffer? Uncovering the Hidden Dynamics of Human Nature

90. Your Full Potential: How to Overcome Fear and Solve Any Problem

91. Your Soul Purpose: Reincarnation and the Spectrum of Consciousness in Human Evolution

About the Publisher

This book was published by 22 Lions Publishing.

www.22Lions.com